D1411680

STOP THINKING:
HOW TO BREAK FREE FROM DEPRESSION AND ANXIETY TWO MINUTES AT A TIME

ROB BROYLES

BALBOA.PRESS
A DIVISION OF HAY HOUSE

Balboa Press books may be ordered through booksellers or by contacting:

Balboa Press
A Division of Hay House
1663 Liberty Drive
Bloomington, IN 47403
www.balboapress.com
844-682-1282

Because of the dynamic nature of the Internet, any web addresses or links contained in this book may have changed since publication and may no longer be valid. The views expressed in this work are solely those of the author and do not necessarily reflect the views of the publisher, and the publisher hereby disclaims any responsibility for them.

The author of this book does not dispense medical advice or prescribe the use of any technique as a form of treatment for physical, emotional, or medical problems without the advice of a physician, either directly or indirectly. The intent of the author is only to offer information of a general nature to help you in your quest for emotional and spiritual well-being. In the event you use any of the information in this book for yourself, which is your constitutional right, the author and the publisher assume no responsibility for your actions.

Any people depicted in stock imagery provided by Getty Images are models, and such images are being used for illustrative purposes only.
Certain stock imagery © Getty Images.

Print information available on the last page.

ISBN: 979-8-7652-3420-4 (sc)
ISBN: 979-8-7652-3421-1 (e)

Balboa Press rev. date: 09/07/2022

To my wonderful children, Nick and Hannah, I dedicate this book to you. It is with the greatest love that I write this - with the hope that you will never need it. This is the story about my journey to complete fulfillment.

I will share the way I found the following:

- How to know what you want
- How to make decisions - even those with conflicting and confusing outcomes
- How to know when you have done enough work to let yourself rest
- How to know you are on the right path for your life
- How to free yourself from anxiety, depression, and negative emotions
- How to get better sleep
- How to stop an overthinking mind
- How to find the right career path
- How to deal with unpleasant situations
- How to change your eating habits
- How to enjoy exercise
- For the workaholic, how to rest
- For the relaxed person, how to accomplish big goals
- How to make working hard feel effortless
- How to enjoy brief moments without worry
- How to make sure you go to Heaven

TABLE OF CONTENTS

Prelude ix

Chapter 1:   What It Means to Stop Thought 1

Chapter 2:   Align Your Mind 13

Chapter 3:   Align Your Body 18

Chapter 4:   Baseline 21

Chapter 5:   Addictions 27

Chapter 6:   The World is a Dream 31

Chapter 7:   Black Sky 34

Chapter 8:   Food for Thought 37

Chapter 9:   Energy Depletion 40

Chapter 10:   Change Your Thoughts, Change the World 45

Chapter 11:   Inside an Anxious Mind 47

Chapter 12:   Evicting Anxiety 50

Chapter 13:   Vibrational Pull 55

Chapter 14:   Flowing Energy 59

Chapter 15:   The Runaway Mind 61

Chapter 16:   Joe & God 64

Chapter 17:   Merging Worlds 69

Chapter 18:   Everywhere I Go, I Am 75

Chapter 19:   Running Away, Standing Still, or Running Towards 79

Chapter 20:   Peace vs. Worldly Treasures 85

Chapter 21:   What's Next? 88

Chapter 22:   Personal Guide & Protector 97

Chapter 23:   Shifting Through Technology 99

Chapter 24:   Breaking Dysfunctional Mind Patterns 104

Chapter 25:   Struggle vs. Allow 108

Chapter 26:   Insanity 124

Chapter 27:   New Boundaries & New Freedoms 126

Chapter 28:   The Choice 130

Chapter 29:   Belief 139

Chapter 30:   Balance 144

Chapter 31:   I Am & I Do 151

Chapter 32:   Our Path 158

Chapter 33:   Lost & Found 163

Chapter 34:   Being the Light as an Empath 167

Chapter 35:   Recognizing The Ego 169

Chapter 36:   My Pep Talk to You 174

Epilogue 179

PRELUDE

I have written this book from the only perspective I know - mine. It is through our unfiltered unique expression, in total alignment with God that we will find what our heart is searching for. The specific details in this book are less important to grasp than understanding the details of one's own unique character, what makes you - you. If you find I have repeated myself or have capitalized certain words referring to a higher power, it was intentional. Without the experience, words mean nothing. The examples, analogies, and metaphors used within this book fall incredibly short of being a complete and whole description. They only point the way and are not a true bellwether to base your own forward progress upon. Instead, try to imagine what it is that I am attempting to convey rather than getting caught up in the lexicon. Words are just pointing the way. I am eager to convey what I have discovered.

When aligned with Source, fear steps aside and worry moves away. Anxiety turns and runs. Negative energy is shown the exit. Night becomes day. Misery is gone. Insomnia disappears. Depression becomes swallowed by the light. The label "chronic, severe anxiety" becomes a thing of the past. These distant memories still exist, but the pain is no longer felt. I was a different person in my youth. I was not me. Labels only disguise your true self. You only require one label standing on one emotional foundation - that label is God's child, and the emotional foundation is peace. You are not your name, race, religion, or job title. You are not the thoughts of lack or struggle that creep into your head. You are blessed, whole, abundant, and secure. You are at peace, even when life's challenges arise. Why?

Because the same divine essence that makes up who you are, holds these challenges in its control.

Neither the information in this book, nor any other approach, is capable of anything other than helping you look inward to find your own specific expression of Universal Consciousness. No method will perfectly click with you unless it is your own. Finding yourself is freedom and is actually the source of our happiness. Following a religious tradition or the method within this book is fine for a short time, but modalities only point to the path someone else took. It is imperative to understand that our physical differences separate us in only the way the hand is not the same as the foot. In the very same way that blood nourishes both the hand and the foot, Universal Consciousness is the connection that all humans have together. It is up to each of us to determine our own path to enlightenment, our own path to true discovery. You will be ready to take a step forward in your own journey when you feel this peace within.

It is only our physical form, our appearance, and our thoughts that separate us from one another. We all share a divine essence as our roots. Outward appearances, and even our thoughts, may be in stark contrast from one another, but those differences are smoke and mirrors. Every person on the planet has a different face and yet is spiritually borne from the same divine essence. There is a connection between all of us - that connection is God, Universal Consciousness, Source Energy, or whatever name you label it. We all come from the same divine bloodline, so to speak. Part of the act of alignment is to quiet the mind and remove our individual judgments and labels. This enables you to see the world of contrast and differences as a light of oneness and unity. Alignment allows you to remove anything that might restrict you from seeing the divine essence in all people and things. When we know ourselves so deeply as to remove even our thoughts, we are then able to connect our individual expression of Consciousness to the One Consciousness. By doing so, one has everything necessary. Nothing is missing. The light removes the darkness, and we see clearly.

Chapter One
WHAT IT MEANS TO
STOP THOUGHT

In order for you to come to a state of awareness and live from an inner state of abundance, you must first understand the term "no thought." The connection between our thoughts and our level of anxiety is profound. We truly become the thoughts we think. Once you recognize that you have tied complaints, judgments, and labels to what you once thought were productive thoughts, you will be set free. Inside the stillness of no thought will arise wisdom and thus, will generate physical action that can be taken from a universal and creative standpoint. Rarely are new and creative actions taken while under the influence of your subconscious, habitual mind patterns.

Imagine you are in bed. It is two o'clock in the morning and you are awakened by an unfamiliar sound coming from another part of the house. It is pitch black as you listen carefully to hear where the next sound might come from. You wonder if it is a burglar. You are not thinking about the past or future. You deliberately stop all thoughts and listen very closely. You listen with all of your senses on high alert. That is an example of no thought. It is a deliberate act of stopping thought, but also being wide awake and alert at the same time. That state of mind is what you will want to practice as often as you can, without the intrusions of other thoughts or emotions during meditation.

Imagine being on high alert while waiting for something pleasant like a surprise birthday party. You are waiting with great suspense for the guest of honor to arrive. At that moment of anticipation, the mind is not automatically active with useless worry or habitual autopilot-type thoughts. The mind is not describing anything or complaining to you. These are two different examples of no thought, illustrating a sense of urgency and alertness all the while deliberately stopping all thoughts.

The emotions of fear or jubilation have no place in your mind when in a state of no thought. The only emotion that arises from no thought should be one of peaceful alertness. As with a party, you might be on high alert because you cannot wait to give the honored guest the birthday present. Perhaps this "waiting" period consists of an egoic drive to give the best gift, which is certainly not the emotion of divine peace. This is why examples of the heightened state of alertness can be very misleading. The reason I share examples of erroneous levels of alertness is because many have no idea what it means to stop thought. This mental state of mind, filled with rest and peace, simply does not exist for many people. Most have no idea how to find the peace that passes all understanding within this "stillness."

Many of us have experienced moments of "time standing still." When my son and I went skydiving we both felt this sensation. A feeling of clarity arises as the brain completely stops its conditioned and habitual patterns of thought. A high degree of alertness becomes the present state of mind.

I remember a few other moments when time seemed to stand still for me. The destruction of my egoic, habitual nature began when I saw my wife of seventeen years with someone else. This disaster coincided with my ego shattering within me. As I watched them together, my mental focus acutely sharpened. I heard the sound of my own heart beating as if it were coming out of my chest. I truly thought my heart was beating louder than normal and the two of them would hear my heart beating as I watched. I thought the sound of my heart would alert them that they had been caught.

I did not know it then, but my heart was not actually beating louder. It was my focus that actually sharpened, and I became on high alert. My ears picked up sounds that are normally concealed by our day-to-day thinking. This immediately shocked me back into the present moment. I could barely breathe. I lost my appetite for about six months and felt as if a huge part of my insides were ripped out.

I pointed the finger of blame back then, but I now realize the pain and loss I felt was from the ego's exposure to the light of Consciousness. It felt heart wrenching, but it turned out to be the best thing that ever happened to me. I became free of the destructive ego's quiet and secret leadership within me. I had a glimpse into the heightened state of awareness that I would later use to notice the sky, the clouds, the tree, the river, and all of my surroundings with.

When I quiet my thoughts with purpose and intention, I find clarity and peace. I know all is well. I have been able to take this place of mental freedom with me wherever I go. Another way of saying this is, "I am" this mental place of freedom now. You can also attain peace. If you do not know how, rest assured, you will get there. You just need to start somewhere. That is why I have given these examples, however, do not search for a specific feeling. Try to find the place of peace within you that resembles "home" to you or at least a home that you have always dreamed of.

Stopping thought simply means becoming highly alert and attentive to your surroundings, but without labeling them. Describing your surroundings does not take you deeper. Again, no thought means no thoughts, but an enhanced awareness of your surroundings goes hand-in-hand with the act of no thought. Sometimes I use the ringing in my ears to help me quiet my mind. The tinnitus used to be annoying. Now it takes me deeper into a mental place of peace. The mind's way of saying thank you for taking it off the habitual treadmill of active thoughts is to send the feeling of peace when it is still and at rest. This wonderful, mental place of serenity with no highs or lows became a replacement for "things." I noticed the short-lived feelings that come with every worldly gain. A new bike, new relationship, or new this or that, all pale in comparison to being comfortable in my own skin. I am home and you can be too.

I do think peace is the abstract thing we all crave, but many do not know they are even looking for it. They continue to seek pleasure from material, worldly objects with the hope that one day that car, house, or relationship will give them what their inside is devoid of. They continue on this hamster wheel without ever truly "waking up" to this fact. Many are in the seeking mode, and will be for life, always thinking one day it will come and denying the freedom within. Not being able to find the peace that passes all understanding has no reflection on you, your value, or your worth. If you have not found peace within, accept this fact. When you do, you may just actually find it. That is the trick. It will always be right where you least expect it. Do not think about it. Just experience it. "Try" to find it, and you might just miss it.

Peace resides in the mental place of rest. To the active mind, this is absurd. Comparing ourselves to a tree seems absurd to the active and thinking mind but take a moment to be open to this analogy and it may help you to understand. The tree is at peace and at rest. The sky is at peace and at rest. The bumble bee, flapping its wings a million miles per hour is at rest. The bee is pollinating flowers and contributing to the world, all the while being in a state of rest. Does the eagle soaring above us appear effortless, or in a state of struggle? Obviously, the eagle is in a mental state of rest. The tree provides a home to animals and cleans the air we breathe. It also provides beauty. All of this is done from a place of peace and rest. The eagle makes its own contributions to the world all the while staying in a mental place of rest.

Imagine the eagle comparing itself to an elephant, becoming jealous, and trying to walk the earth instead of flying. Imagine the bumble bee getting angry that another bee just took his flower, so it destroys the flower that the other bee is pollinating. Nature does just fine without egoic contributions of distrust, jealousy, and so on. Humans suffer from a mental disease that is completely unbeknownst to them. It is laced with fear and negativity, and it will destroy the planet if we do not wake up. Nature will evolve just fine without humans' need to cover up, hide, and operate from a false, mental state of insufficiency. You are already enough. There is no need to "try" at anything. You can be you. You do not have to pretend to be something you are not. The tree in the woods is not complaining because of the weight of the snow on its branches. You do not have to feel this negativity if you accept what the ego wants to complain about. It is our refusal to accept things as they are, that causes suffering. Stopping the thoughts will open the door to freedom for you. This must be done over and over until the mind's habitual patterns are broken. It will take mental work. It will require you to do something you have, quite possibly, never done - that is to relax in knowing that all is well. That statement sounds frightening to the ego as the spirit senses a celebration on the horizon.

Another way to look at the idea of no thought is through the following analogy. Our vision can be narrowly focused on one point, or we can widen our view peripherally. When people are under the habitual influences of the conditioned mind, their view of the world and their thoughts are squeezed into a narrow frame that is determined by the ego. To view your world peripherally, you must be alert and aware of your general surroundings without labels, judgments, and complaints. At the same time, you will notice the specific world around you.

Imagine walking down the street and a beautiful shadow of peace and security walks with you everywhere you go. Notice how your mind is aware of this shadow of peace while you are crossing the street. Notice this shadow of peace as you are getting ready for bed. Everywhere you go and in everything you do; you are consciously aware of this wonderful, divine entity that is always with you. This is a form of peripheral awareness. When in a state of mental peace, the mind has no thoughts, but it is also highly aware of a wonderful sense of peace.

When we stop our thoughts, we interrupt the broken record that plays on repeat in the subconscious mind. It recorded the time you were hurt many moons ago, buried the emotion under a layer of the false self, and it attempted to protect you by assuming every similar event will cause you harm. We have a thousand of these so-called "protective services" going on inside our heads. We know this because they themselves are the ones causing the fear, anxiety, and negativity. We also have this hidden entity serving up a platter of so-called "good for you" events. These are the events that stroked the ego as a youngster or possibly as an adult. When we received what we thought was love by following the orders of well-meaning, but egoically driven others, we received an accolade. We learned that we win the approval of others by doing this or that, but not by following our own heart's divine desires.

If you are a person driven by the ego, you will need these accolades. You do not realize the accolades you chase are bottomless, and you will continue to find your place in life by stroking the ego, never once realizing you are not following your God-given path for life. The ego will direct you to do this or that to feel good. When we stop thoughts, we see the ego for what it is. We are able to notice that the things we thought were bringing us temporary pleasure were not even part of our divine purpose. They were attempts to seek pleasure through the act of pleasing others, and what others felt we should do or be, and we had no clue.

Stopping thoughts brings clarity. It also brings an epiphany. I eventually woke up from the egoic disease of hidden deception about my true identity. When the room stopped spinning, I slept well, ate well, my digestive tract worked well, and I found out that all is well! I asked myself, "Who told me I was insufficient and needed to feel anxiety?" One sure sign that you are following the orders of the undetectable ego is by the way you feel. If you deeply sense the lows of life as if you are being torn apart at every loss, or if you intensely feel you have finally made it at the wins of life, you may be under the influence of the undetectable ego.

It all comes down to whose influence you are under and how you feel. If you are devastated over a challenging event, to the point of it causing you to become immobilized, you may have your identity tied up in the ego. On the other hand, if you desperately place all your worth in your achievements, you might be under the influence of the ego. If either of those scenarios seem perfectly acceptable to you, you might be under the influence of the ego.

There is absolutely no need to become immobilized because of life's challenges, and conversely, there is absolutely no need to feel bad about yourself because you have not accomplished something. You are already enough. You are more than enough. If life does not feel like a giant playground and you do not feel like the star performing actor or actress, then you might just be under the influence of the ego. If you are upset that you just found out that you have been under the influence of the ego for the first several years of your life, you might be under the influence of the ego. If you feel guilty, you might be under the influence of the ego.

The ego operates in a world of comparisons and complaints. The person free of the ego is free indeed. You will know when you have dropped the ego because you will no longer ask or wonder about it. When the thoughts are stopped, we become free to follow the divine light of Consciousness and act from a life of peace and harmony as a co-creator of love. There is no need to wonder if acting from a place of true and divine no thought gives a license to others to misbehave. If they are aligned, they are on the same path of love as you.

Some changes will take place as you stop thoughts and become aligned to Source Energy, the One Consciousness, or God, whichever name you prefer. You will not be asked to give up desirable things. Your desires will change. You will desire to eat well and do other good things without struggling with your willpower to bring them to fruition.

Most forms of irrelevant thought are habitual. They are commonly derived from the past. Conditioning and paradigms play a large part in our daily thoughts. Mental thoughts will actually lead a person to a physical and material destination. Our thoughts are what have gotten us to where we are today, good or bad. It was your thoughts that helped you get the job, the house, and so on. Thoughts come with emotions and just the thought of doing something, depending on the emotion attached to it, will guide us from a conditioned, habitual standpoint. In other words, we will stay away or gravitate to the same things that we did in the past. By doing so, we could be making wrong choices or even feeling invalid emotions about a particular subject.

My opinion regarding certain circumstances in the past have changed as an adult. I may have had views that were correct from the standpoint of years and years ago, but the thoughts were completely unfounded as an adult. I did not notice that I was being steered by my own misconceptions. Some habitual thoughts have gone into the subconscious and tied to these thoughts, are emotions from the past. Emotions linked to a past thought or memory, are experienced by the body in much the same way the actual event, say twenty-five years ago, may have stirred the same emotion. The body does not know the difference between the emotion it felt years ago from the emotion it is currently feeling as those same memories are brought up. The body thinks the actual event is happening again through the emotional rise that is triggered by your thoughts. This matters because subconscious, habitual thoughts will create a rise in emotions during any part of the day. Without your awareness of them, you may feel whatever it is that the unbridled mind stirs up, even if it is false. Anxiety used to consume me. For no reason at all, I would be overcome with fear and panic. I used to relate my anxiety to any random circumstance that was happening at the moment. I would then steer clear of the situation because

I wrongly thought that it was what was sparking the anxiety. After learning to quiet my mind, the panic attacks dissipated, and the insomnia became less and less.

Negative, hidden thoughts will stir up emotions all on their own without anything to substantiate it. Suddenly, I thought that this was a message from God warning me to make a change in my life. I really had no idea what was going on. Back then, I did not know God directs us through love and peace, not fear. Out of the blue, with no outer threat, I would feel anxious. Years before I began this practice of self-awareness, I would look to my physical environment for something that caused this fear in me. I would ask myself, "Was there something I did wrong? Am I facing imminent harm?" If I saw no immediate threat, I would search for something that must have stirred up such a ferocious, negative feeling, never once thinking that the emotion was flawed. I might decide the negative emotion was a signal, warning me that I said the wrong thing to a friend or that I should be nervous about an upcoming test in school.

Having the notion that the negative emotions inside me were produced by something other than the physical realm (e.g., either past, present, or future) would be my biggest hurdle to overcome. I believed wholeheartedly that this negative emotion was real and present. I believed, in some cases, it was some sort of warning signal from God to make a drastic change in my life. I thought it was a message to help me in some way.

Obviously, panic attacks arising from subconscious, habitual thoughts developed as a child, can wreak havoc on a person's life. Quieting the mind allows the body to return to equilibrium. It also brings clarity to the moment. With practice, if you quiet the mind often, you will be able to do so during one of these panic attacks. The doorway to freedom from panic attacks is opened even through short meditations of no thought. You can be sure that the anxiety you feel will become less and less as time goes on.

I can now say that I no longer suffer from panic attacks or anxiety, although I do have negative emotions arise from time to time. I am able to allow these feelings rather than resist them and they dissipate in no time at all. For those of us finally free of anxiety, it is just as important to free the mind from habitual thoughts. Even the healthiest individuals have hidden thoughts that steer their conscious lives from a place of unknowing. You may have learned a behavior from a circumstance as a child that does not serve you well as an adult. The behavior may be a result of a circumstance that continues in your adult life. You are likely making choices, and acting on an unsubstantiated pattern, that has no validity in your present moment. You will not know this until the mind is still. These revelations will come as you practice quieting your mind.

Unsubstantiated, subconscious feelings that arise from historical events sometimes steal our moments of joy. As a kid I was bullied. It was not until I quieted my mind as an adult that I realized I was carrying around feelings that people disliked me. I was naturally an introvert. I always had a low-level of uneasiness when around other people. This did not wreck my life, but it points to the importance of practicing a quiet mind. Perhaps I would have participated in more social events if I uncovered the source of my unease earlier in my life. You do not necessarily need to know the "why" behind what you do. You just need to quiet the mind, and through that silence, wisdom will emerge. I say that to point out the obvious. Life can be so different when the subconscious conditioning of the past is removed. It is not as important to know why you are afraid of public speaking, afraid of anything, or even excellent at something - it is more important to remove the conditioned self. The reasoning will come later.

Science tells us we have over 65,000 thoughts rolling around in our head during the course of one day. We do not need to discover the importance of each thought. We need to practice stopping thought, just for a short time at first, even if it is just for two minutes per day. When you are first getting started, the end goal of no thought is actually not as important as the significance of simply taking up the practice. When you take time out of your day to practice this, you are practicing taking control away from the ego. The ego is what runs on autopilot in the back of our mind, interfering with our lives. The ego is very clever. More than likely, you have no idea the ego is running your life until you are able to quiet the mind.

We are basically returning ownership of the mind back to conscious control and therefore, to Consciousness itself. In this way, the past memories and the future thoughts are eliminated from steering our present moment. The memories are still there, but the emotions from the past that dictated that a person is shy, directionally challenged, no good at math, etcetera, will not keep us on the same path. Also, the egoic patterns of dysfunctional versions of self-pride are eliminated. This is just as important as removing self-deprecating thoughts. If you subconsciously think you are good at something when you are not, this practice will return you to a state of mind that is aligned with the creative powers of Source. From there, the fruitfulness of life will occur. This gives rise to the possibility to step outside of the predetermined set of boundaries that once defined you. We have all experienced our taste buds changing as we age. You might enjoy eating something now that you disliked as a child. This also applies to these invisible barriers of personal identification with shyness, public speaking, and so on. The subconscious thought patterns, and the emotions tied to them, will restrict you. For example, if as a child you were ridiculed in front of your class, you might not pursue public speaking. It may not be that you dislike public speaking, you may be exceptional at it. The problem is not the public speaking at all. It is the subconscious thought and emotion that you are still carrying with you on the inside.

Our possibilities are endless. We feel as if we have barriers because we are slaves to the ego that is dripping wet with fear. We have an invisible barrier set up around us in an attempt, from the ego, to protect us. Once the mind is quieted and the body returns to a state of homeostasis, these invisible barriers are removed. Life will improve dramatically. Subconscious and self-destructive behaviors, no matter how big or small, will drop away. Over-eating, insomnia, depression, anxiety, fear, and so on cannot survive in the light of truth. Thus begins the separation process from alignment with the ego and brings alignment with Source Energy to its fruition.

This realignment to Source Energy is where we belong. All sorts of wonderful things begin to happen. The body has more energy because its energy reserves are not wasted on pointless fear. Realignment unlocks the notion of having more time. Each and every moment is felt in a deeper and clearer way. The five senses seem heightened. A channel, of sorts, is opened up to wisdom that did not seem to be there before. Trust is formed on the deepest level between your own individual emanation of Source Energy and its connection to the same Source Energy that is found in all things.

A feeling of fulfillment and contentment will be realized in all areas of your life, including places you may have felt incomplete prior to alignment. This "need" of the physical world to be something other than what it is not, disappears. The body becomes lighter, and a healing presence is felt. A vibration of love is emitted.

These wonderful shifts may occur for just a short time during the quiet and still practice. The body might return to disharmony shortly after your two minutes of practice. That is okay. For me, it took an enormous amount of tenacity to make the shift to where I have more moments of alignment to Source, than not. I remember lying in bed, trembling after I started this practice. The insomnia got worse as the ego fearfully screamed within the dark corners of my mind. At first, this felt like torture.

I felt like an alcoholic losing their best friend, alcohol. My abuser, the ego, was shouting at me that I was making a mistake by not listening to it anymore. The ego had been my dysfunctional best friend and a great security blanket for the majority of my life. It took a lot of mental work on my part. Turns out, the mental work did not physically tax me and it was an invaluable means to freedom. The obligation is on the individual to find this freedom. The ego may want a pill, a step-by-step guide, or something else to do the work. Do not listen to it. Practice calming the mind until you can laugh at the voice of the ego.

Not long after, came a shift in perception. The old me, that was aligned with the ego, saw difficulties in others. I am not sure how to explain it, but I used to feel pity for others when I thought they were missing out on something. If I saw a homeless person I would say under my breath, "Aw, that poor man," or when talking with a cashier complaining about her troubled life, I might let her know that I was feeling sorry for her. I do not see the obvious physical and negative traits of people and situations as much anymore. Instead, I see their potential. I see their blessings.

Now, when I look at the world, I see possibility and love. I am not sure what to call it. From this new perspective, I might say to the cashier, "Ma'am, everything will work out for the best and I know you are in the good hands of God." I certainly would not align with the fear of the ego in response to anything anymore. I do not feel pity anymore and I certainly would not say, "Oh you poor thing." That seems to steal a person's ability to crawl out of their own desperate hole. To say something like, "Things are changing for the better," aligns with Source and sends a vibration of love.

An overwhelming feeling of gratefulness will materialize as an appreciation for just being alive overflows every cell of the body. The old me dreamed of a bucket list of items to complete before life's end. After aligning with Source, I have actually said under my breath, "At this very moment, I feel complete." The new bucket list, if you will, has no physical places or accomplishments written on it. Although, traveling and doing this or that would be a wonderful bonus to life, the only thing I absolutely desire is the wonderful feeling of completeness that comes with alignment to Source. The best part is that this peaceful state of mind can be obtained at any moment through alignment.

Without quieting the mind, the hidden, egoic, fearful leader leaves an individual feeling incomplete. It is through this lack of completeness that you will strive to find answers or even find yourself in the physical and tangible world. Once alignment to Source is made, however short of a glimpse it may be, you realize that the physical and tangible world cannot provide anything sustainable. While it is true there is food and water in the physical realm, true sustainment of inner peace cannot be found here. As a matter of fact, nothing truly good is ever lost while traversing life and fine-tuning alignment. Contrary to the ego, everything is gained while in alignment.

There are five steps to free yourself from anxiety.

1. Break the habitual stream of thoughts.
2. Understand that it is the thoughts themselves that are habitual, living in your subconscious mind.
3. Separate your labels and judgment from what you feel are considered important thoughts.
4. Introduce space (or a gap) in the habitual patterns of dysfunctional thoughts (i.e., notice how long you can go without negative thought patterns).
5. Allow new, creative, and thus, aligned thoughts to develop from the depths of divine wisdom.

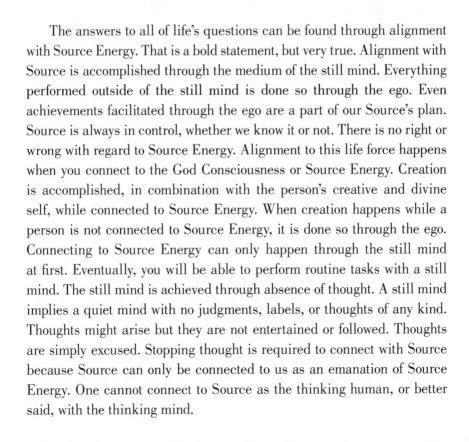

Chapter Two

ALIGN YOUR MIND

The answers to all of life's questions can be found through alignment with Source Energy. That is a bold statement, but very true. Alignment with Source is accomplished through the medium of the still mind. Everything performed outside of the still mind is done so through the ego. Even achievements facilitated through the ego are a part of our Source's plan. Source is always in control, whether we know it or not. There is no right or wrong with regard to Source Energy. Alignment to this life force happens when you connect to the God Consciousness or Source Energy. Creation is accomplished, in combination with the person's creative and divine self, while connected to Source Energy. When creation happens while a person is not connected to Source Energy, it is done so through the ego. Connecting to Source Energy can only happen through the still mind at first. Eventually, you will be able to perform routine tasks with a still mind. The still mind is achieved through absence of thought. A still mind implies a quiet mind with no judgments, labels, or thoughts of any kind. Thoughts might arise but they are not entertained or followed. Thoughts are simply excused. Stopping thought is required to connect with Source because Source can only be connected to us as an emanation of Source Energy. One cannot connect to Source as the thinking human, or better said, with the thinking mind.

Although we are a part of Source, we cannot make the divine connection of knowledge and wisdom through thought. Our clever, ever-thinking mind cannot fathom infinity with no beginning or end. It is not possible to align our finite and limited brain with the infinite Universal Consciousness. That would be like trying to read a book with our tongue or hear music with our nose. Only the correct medium will align with Source however, Source is always aligned with us. We cannot break the connection. We can only stop listening. We have the capacity to connect our consciousness with Universal Consciousness through the stillness of the mind.

Consciousness cannot be understood intellectually. It cannot be made into something the mind can understand. Consciousness is a different realm or dimension that the mind is incapable of understanding. We can, however, quiet our mind, be conscious and awake with no thought, and make this alignment with Source Energy.

Connection to Source is not accomplished through the ego. While we can manifest and create on the egoic level without alignment, the culmination of events would not be made in conjunction with Source. However, Source creates with the help of humans whether we want to be a part of it, or not. In other words, humans can create without the help of Source, but Source always creates through humans, whether we are aware of it, or not. The still mind is achieved through multiple avenues. Only one of which will align an individual with Universal Consciousness. For example, some may resort to alcohol to quiet their mind. This does not facilitate the same type of vibration where Source Energy resides. Drinking alcohol exists on a low frequency where thought is slowed and the mind becomes still, but the mind cannot transmit or receive on that frequency. Source does not operate there. Source operates on a higher vibration.

Another example of quieting the mind is when we participate in extreme sports. A person's thoughts are slowed or even stopped when engaging in an extreme sport where death may be the possible outcome of a minor mistake. There is no time for thinking when riding a motorcycle at 200 MPH. Reactions must be automatic at these speeds. Taking the time to think about how much acceleration should be applied in the corner may cost one his/her life. I was attracted to extreme sports because it took my mind off anxious thoughts in a way I was unable to do by myself.

No labels, judgments, paradigms, or past conditioning exist in the mind during extreme sports.

While it is good practice to align with Source moment by moment - and this is actually the goal - most will find it difficult to perform tasks while simultaneously being in alignment. There are different degrees of alignment intensity. When we are able to be physically and completely still, it is much more possible to devote an enormous amount of conscious energy into alignment. It is also possible to be in alignment while multitasking, however the level of intensity will diminish the more we focus on other missions. Once the task is completed, we can devote more intensity to alignment. Another way of describing alignment while going about your daily activities is to become immersed so deeply in an activity that judgments, labels, worries, and so on, do not creep into the mind.

You can be aligned while performing extreme sports, in the sense that unnecessary thoughts are stopped, but the alignment is usually the byproduct of the activity and not done with purpose. The still mind that vibrates on the same frequency as Source has no agenda. The still mind vibrating on the frequency of Source desires nothing. Quieting the mind can be accomplished through a breathing exercise while meditating. The still mind can be accomplished even while performing a chore or task, but some people will need the help of meditation when getting started. Through the practice of no thought, one will eventually be able to do all things while aligned and without the hindrance of irrelevant thoughts. Irrelevant thoughts are thoughts that have nothing to do with alignment. Worry or consideration given to any thought that does not pertain to the present moment are considered irrelevant.

No thought may be easier to attain when focusing on your breath. It is accomplished in accordance with all five senses though - touch, taste, sound, smell, and sight. While lying or sitting in a comfortable position, close your eyes and use all five senses, including sight. While the eyes are closed, sense any light that might be filtering through. With the eyes closed, if it is completely dark and no spots or shadows of light are detected, simply notice the vast darkness. Use all the other senses to detect your surroundings. Notice the way the different parts of the body feel as they touch the surfaces you are lying or sitting on. Notice the sounds. Is there a clock ticking? Are there birds singing outside? Do you smell anything?

The goal is to allow the mind to rest so that it no longer seeks habitual thoughts of labeling and complaining.

As you are redirecting the mind to the body, you may notice changes taking place. The mind does not think on autopilot. You are taking control, albeit ever so slightly. This allows you to take the reins back. The more this is practiced in calm times, the more likely you will develop the ability to do this with your eyes open during more difficult circumstances and eventually, all day long. Remember, absence of thought means no dramatization about the present moment, no references to the past or future, and no judgments or labels.

It is important not to label or judge anything, especially during this meditation. Try to focus the mind on the body's senses without commentary. Do not follow or entertain thoughts that describe anything other than facts. For instance, do not follow a thought that describes something in the form of a complaint. I use the ringing in my ears as a method of alignment also. By listening to the ringing in the ears rather than trying not to hear the ringing, I am allowing the moment and bringing in alignment.

Stick to facts like, I hear a dog barking, that smells like bread baking, or my breathing is slow. The pleasant senses should not be dramatically described either. In this way, you are taking control away from the mind's habitual patterns of thinking of the past or future; labeling or judging; and making a big deal out of nothing.

This is good foundational work because eventually this is the way in which you will want to function in the world. The less the mind describes events in a grandiose way, the more conscious you will be, thereby allowing you to align with Source. Remember that it is through alignment that you become the co-creator to creation and manifestation. The only agenda is to be aligned as often as possible and hopefully, always.

The mind will most likely dislike this control. I had an overactive mind that stirred up thoughts to the point that I was diagnosed with severe, chronic anxiety. I was unable to get my mind to focus on breathing at first. Eventually, I used a two-minute timer to help alleviate my mind's resistance. For some reason, my mind was okay with stopping thought for just two minutes. It was not okay with stopping thought for an unknown amount of time. The ego in me would try and tell me that this practice was stupid. It would say things like, "You have bills to pay." It would remind me that the so-called real-world stuff is more important than stopping thought. It would tell me that I might miss out on something important if I stopped thought. Eventually, the egoic mind inside me allowed me to stop thinking, but only if I had a timer set for just two minutes. This was the beginning of the downfall of egoic suffering for me. My anxiety's days were finally numbered.

After a few weeks of practice, I was eventually able to get my mind to focus on breathing for the entire two minutes. I would continue to take this two-minute practice into multiple periods throughout the day. I would practice this morning, noon, and night, eventually extending the time frame from minutes into hours.

The more I practiced this, the more I was able to stop thought without focusing on the body's senses. I would even be able to stop thought in the middle of challenges that would typically stir up anxiety in me. I was starting to become free.

Chapter Three

ALIGN YOUR BODY

After aligning the mind to Source, the body needs to be aligned.

Focusing on the body's five senses is a great way to bring our mind to a place of no thought and ultimately to a place of alignment. After two minutes of practice turns to five minutes and five minutes turns to hours, soon you will find yourself able to be in this place of no thought for days at a time. A new habit is formed and most importantly, a new way of life will emerge. The body has now become a place of "outer" focus to stabilize the mind. After this new, healthy habit is formed on the physical level, you must practice noticing the way your inner body feels physically and make mental or physical adjustments to realign the body to Source.

Once the mind's random thoughts are noticed, calmed, and guided towards loving thoughts, the same must be done with the body. Starting with two minutes at a time, pay attention to your body. Start anywhere you like. If you have a physical area of weakness or illness, start there. By placing mental attention to your body through the act of awareness, your body will give you clues to the exact spot where negative energy is stored and needs to be released. Unlike in the physical realm where a "cure," pill, or form of therapy, is needed to relieve pain, nothing other than awareness is necessary. Paying close, mental attention to all areas of the body is enough to start the healing process.

Healing my spinal injury is an example of this. Years of tension stored in my lower back, in the form of negative energy, contributed to painful osteoarthritis. The physical pain in my spine was a result of ignoring and resisting life energy. The reason behind why we resist, allowing energy to move through us, is not important now. We need to stop the bleeding before we can pursue who shot us. The path of discovery should be in the form of awareness first. The details will come later.

After some time, you will develop a remarkable sensitivity to your body, and incredibly, your life's direction will be found within. You no longer have to live with your pain. The goal is to live a life in harmony with Consciousness. Continually ignoring small areas of discomfort will lead to major injuries. Escalation of discomfort and pain is part of evolution and is a signal to return the body back to its natural state of alignment and balance.

It is possible to take the body to the grave in complete disregard for its natural state of peace and comfort. Ignoring the body's pain leads to the need for more and more outside help like medications or therapy. The first half of my life, I ignored my body because I thought it was macho or heroic to do so. Unfortunately, I passed this trait on to my children.

The second half of my life's journey is different. My children are adults now and my best attempt to pass along knowledge for a life of peace is through this book. Ignoring the body's small signals of discomfort is fine for a short time, but it cannot be sustained. Ignoring these small signs will result in high blood pressure, anxiety, insomnia, depression, overeating, and so on. There is a peaceful and easy way to live life. The harmonious life, lived in connection to Source Energy, is the most rewarding and pleasing life there is.

The body's inner signals of discomfort and peace can be used as a road map for life. This means a person can, and should, follow their own unique set of emotional and physical DNA. This DNA is designed specifically for you as a guide to traverse life. Using this knowledge, you will be able to take the world's laws and rules and marry them with your own inner signal. Following the inner mind and the body's cues does not give you license to break laws. It simply means you should follow these inner barometers as you journey through life.

Most people follow mental conditioning and advice offered from the world. This is fine, but it should come secondary to following your inner mind and body. The world and its rules are a player in the game of life, but to balance the inner mind and body with the outer world is paramount. The world will appear different when you drop your struggles and resistant lifestyle for a life of peace. The tradeoff is that the ego will not know what is going on. Incidentally, it never actually did understand, but that ignorance is also part of the false self.

The world presents some maverick waves from time to time. Just like a proficient surfer, you will be able to ride these waves from a harmonious state of deep peace. The sunbathers on the beach may be perplexed at how adept you are at this. To you, it is not just the only way, but it is the best way. Paying attention to the body is critical as you map the direction for your life. You may have to ignore the ego. If following the ego has been your habit, this may be challenging. I know this to be true of my own life. I have said goodbye to things that served only the ego, but I am much more at peace now.

While aligned, you may not realize a set of specific steps to take in life. This is freedom. While the mind and body are aligned, you will receive the eternal peace that passes all understanding. The long term (and permanent) path or "high road" will be enough to sustain you during the unknown (and temporary) short term periods when you do not feel a strong sense of direction. The power to release the chains of a dysfunctional life lies within you. Mind and body harmony is restored through the internal effort of mind and body alignment.

Chapter Four

BASELINE

Inside all of us is what I call a baseline. It is a vibrational frequency that resonates to the vibration of Universal Consciousness. Every thought and emotion has its own vibrational frequency. Similar to the physical DNA that dictates the physical attributes and so on, the emotional DNA dictates the vibration of harmony we are specifically designed for. In the same way physical DNA dictates our looks and the way we think, emotional DNA dictates our physical world around us based on the vibration we emit. If we drop our emotions to a depressive state, we have dipped below the baseline set for our individual expression of the One Consciousness. Our outer world will reflect that, and depression or anxiety may set in. If we allow our emotions to rise above the baseline of emotional DNA, we become overconfident and/or proud. This also causes suffering. A quest for material objects may reflect one's overconfidence and this is also fleeting.

It is important to note that the emotional rise above or falling below our set baseline is normal. There is no need to control, stop, or suppress emotions. That would be an egoic and futile attempt to change something. It is not our job to suppress emotions. That is a terrible thing to do. Instead, we notice negative energy that stems from the deviation from our baseline and gently guide our thoughts about the situation back in alignment with Source or change our situation. We all have temporary fluctuations in emotions and that is normal. The sign that we have lost our way, is when the emotions have become debilitating. In this way our emotions are not used as something to make a judgment about ourselves, but rather they become the gentle reminders to realign with Source.

A peaceful state of mind is only fulfilled when you live within the baseline of your emotional DNA. Albert Einstein believed that everything in life is vibration. The higher your vibration, the lighter you will feel in your physical, emotional, and mental bodies. Living this way brings alignment with Source Energy. All things are good when one is aligned. All material and worldly circumstances come secondary to alignment. When you are aligned, you live in harmony with the universe. Alignment is a state of mind. It is the practice of living life from a sort of mental perspective of God. From washing the car to paying bills, when one is aligned, peace becomes the foundation for the emotional state of mind. In this way, we put God first in our lives through a mental projection of love for our inner self. We unconditionally love ourselves so much that we purposefully align ourselves to the peace that passes all understanding, no matter the circumstances, or even thoughts, in some cases. Challenges and hardships continue to arise. Working from a mental place of deep-rooted peace allows us to take action to solve problems. If no action can be taken, we can remain at rest from this mental place of peace.

All things manifested, while on your own individual baseline, are created from an internal emotional state of abundance and peace. Things manifested below or above this baseline are created from an emotional state of paucity or insufficiency. The person creating above their baseline is overcompensating for what they think is lacking about themselves. This person may be living an outward life of abundance through great achievements but does so because of an internal feeling of lack. This is not always true, but I make this known for the person who may feel empty inside despite the outward appearance of abundance. The person living their life below the baseline is not living up to his/her God-given potential either. In this case, you may not be creating the physical life you could, due to feelings of insufficiency. These emotional states (above or below the baseline) are usually rooted in fear. Everyone has a different baseline. Some are meant to be athletes, while others are meant to be doctors. Some are completely fulfilled doing what some may consider menial careers. It is not up to others to decide. Suffering occurs if you follow in the footsteps of others, but your emotional baseline DNA is set for something else.

Suffering also occurs if you follow your own God-given baseline but do so feeling negatively about it. For example, if you follow a path, designed by God, but you fear what others think about your path, you are not in alignment to your baseline. In this case, your thoughts are not aligned with your baseline, but your actions are. Thoughts play a larger role in our baseline than our actions. Why? Our thoughts dictate action. Action only comes after the thought. How we feel about something can be entirely incorrect and the paradox is that we place an enormous amount of trust in our thoughts. Alignment will bring clarity to this dilemma.

To follow your baseline completely means to trust in the baseline more than trusting in family, schools, friends, religion, and governments. To become strengthened in the baseline so much so that a person follows their God-given emotional DNA to its fruition, despite what others think, all the while feeling love, bliss, and peace, is Heaven on earth. So, the question remains, how does one do this? Obviously, you need to know what your own emotional DNA baseline is for yourself. You need to learn how to listen to the internal signals that tell you that you have raised above or below the baseline. Finally, you need to emanate your own individual expression of the One Consciousness uniquely without fearing the disapproval of others.

The baseline consists of three levels. Within each level are varying degrees of intensity - above, below, or meeting the baseline. Any one of these three levels is chosen by you, whether you know it or not. If you are raised to think you will never amount to anything, you will choose to believe that. At any given time, you can choose to live your life according to your baseline, but many do not, because they have a stronger belief system in what they see in the material world. They associate truth with the material world. If you have been raised to think you are not smart enough and your grades reflect that, you may believe more in those grades than you do in your own emotional DNA baseline.

The baseline is your inner truth for harmony within the universe. Both thoughts and material manifestations will need to be aligned with the baseline for peace on earth to exist for you. This amounts to Heaven on earth. Every occupation, financial status, family background, and so on has the ability to be in accordance with the baseline - or not. Every variation exists. The poor can be living according to their baseline, or not. A doctor can be living according to his/her baseline, or not. It is not for anyone else to judge. Just as in nature the oak tree will live up to its potential, you can live up to yours. The only difference between you and an oak tree is that you have the freewill to choose *not* to live up to that potential. You have a choice to dislike yourself. A tree cannot. You can choose to be less than your potential. If you have been raised to think less of yourself, you may choose to become less than what the universe has designed for you to become. Of course, many have no choice at all. They are suffering and do not know why. This is because they believe more in their thoughts or actions than they do in their baseline. They may simply not be aware that they have been mentally hijacked by the false and egoic self.

Peace and Heaven on earth are found inside the minds of those who choose to live according to their baseline. They are aligned. Being aligned does not require worldly objects. There is no effort involved - no courses, no classes. You must quiet the mind to get rid of the false self and get to know your true self. Only then will you be at peace. After finding peace within, all of life's challenges are seen as steppingstones to something better, right up until you depart this earth to reenter the loving arms of Source Energy. Some people suffer terribly because they cannot seem to fit in here on earth. Deep down they struggle and desire relief. Sometimes it seems like the more they toughen up and take another difficult step, the more life slaps them in the face.

Living an extended amount of your life above or below the God-given baseline creates stress, anxiety, depression, and suffering. It is normal for people to rise above the baseline in moments of pride, perhaps when they have reached certain milestones. Conversely, it is also normal to dip below the baseline for reasons that may bring on mild cases of depression. I was diagnosed with an anxiety disorder later in my adult life. I lived the first half of my life below the baseline in fear, anxiety, and depression. I attempted to change the way I felt on the inside by living a very physical life - outwardly illustrating my need for an adrenaline rush. I jumped from airplanes, rode motocross, and did rock climbing. My guess is that I tried to convince myself that the frightened little boy inside me did not exist. After many, many years of missing the mark and certainly not living up to my potential or at my baseline, I developed quite a bad habit of being out of alignment.

This habit was formed from years of living from my false self. I lived my life pretending I was not a scared, anxious, depressed person on the inside. I did not do this on purpose. I truly thought I was a brave individual. Deep down there was a small portion of me that noticed the void I was covering up, but I continued to ignore this small sign until it pushed its way to the surface later in life. I suppressed feelings of inadequacy on the inside by acting a certain way on the outside. This led to living a habitual life full of patterns that did not align with my baseline. These patterns developed at a young age. Most of "me" felt fake and I felt like a phony. I never knew why I did not feel authentic until I immersed myself in self-help books, meditation, and the practice of no thought. Turns out, this state of no thought would be the key to all my unanswered questions and release me from the grips of anxiety.

Today, I still enjoy adrenaline-pumping fun like downhill mountain biking, motocross, and skydiving but I do not need those things to feel complete as I once did. The stereotypical man, without an emotional connection, is fading away. Covering up emotions and dealing with pain is a great survival tool if you need to hike forty miles out of the jungle after your plane crashes. Congratulations on having willpower. Short-lived moments of survival are great times to use the strength of your willpower. However, it is not a good way to live one's entire life. The mind and body will break down much faster and almost no lasting relationships will be sustainable. People connect on an emotional level with others. If you are not in touch with your own emotions, you will not be in touch with someone else's. Your relationships will suffer as a result.

I eventually learned how to retrain my brain to be a friend to me. I did not realize how many negative thoughts were habitually being generated by my mind. On this path of self-discovery, I rid myself of anxiety, depression, and insomnia. I learned how to be content and consequently, I developed a better home life, work life, relationships, and even stable finances. The most profound discovery was that there was a mental predisposition inside my own mind that distorted reality. In the same way rose-colored glasses change the colors of the real world, I wore a filter that distorted the perception of the world around me. I saw everything around me as depressing, unfair, and "against" me. I would later discover that my insomnia, fear, anxiety, and depression were the result of mechanisms I created as a child to keep me safe.

After many years of living separate from the God-given baseline for my life; struggle, strain, stress, emotional neglect of self, and anxiety became a normal way of life. That is, of course, until my life fell apart. Living a life outside the baseline is sustainable until death - at which point will end any chance your life can be lived to your fullest potential. You can choose to live in suffering right down to the moment of your demise, or you can choose a life of peace. I did not know I had this choice when I was sleeping just two hours a night and waking up with a racing mind. I did not know I could shut off the mind without alcohol or drugs. I did not know I could be at peace.

It took a divorce, loss of a relationship with my children, depression, anxiety, insomnia, financial hardship, a spinal injury, and immense suffering, to bring me to my knees. I begged and pleaded for God to take away the pain and suffering. Moments of freedom occurred, but it was not until I learned how to stop the racing thoughts in my head that I felt lasting relief. I realized that I had the power to bring peace into my life. I spent my past begging for help when I had the key all along. Imagine a safe place, where no matter what decision you make, where you are, or what is going on around you, you are completely safe and truly abundant. That is alignment. That is living from an inner state of peace, so solid, that nothing rocks your boat.

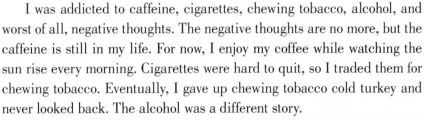

Chapter Five
ADDICTIONS

I was addicted to caffeine, cigarettes, chewing tobacco, alcohol, and worst of all, negative thoughts. The negative thoughts are no more, but the caffeine is still in my life. For now, I enjoy my coffee while watching the sun rise every morning. Cigarettes were hard to quit, so I traded them for chewing tobacco. Eventually, I gave up chewing tobacco cold turkey and never looked back. The alcohol was a different story.

When my life fell apart, I found alcohol to be my reliable, best friend. I call this period "the blessing of my suffering." The addiction to alcohol gave me a bizarre look into what it is like to stop all negative thought. There is no positive value to being drunk. As an alcoholic, I was harming my body, my life, and the people around me. Strangely, my alcoholism did give me something hopeful. It played an important role in showing me what happens when all thought is stopped. I can now see very clearly that my struggle gave me insight into this very blissful moment.

When drunk, I experienced bliss - a sweet, euphoric release. One day, I wondered if I could create this feeling on my own without alcohol. By the time I began this line of questioning, I understood that I had a fairly strong addiction to battle. I could not stop drinking. As a matter of fact, I could not be sober. It was too painful to be sober. I would get terrible headaches and my body would tremble when I started to sober up. I was incapacitated with a spinal injury that was terrifying to me. I was wrong, alcoholism was worse. I remember feeling like I was trapped inside a jailhouse looking out with no escape in sight. Alcohol had its hands wrapped around my throat and I was slowly suffocating.

I was in the throes of something I never felt before. I drank vodka for breakfast, chased by several beers, before the alcohol would finally make me feel "normal." Eventually, I would kick this addiction. The headaches, rage, vomiting, cold sweats, and trembling limbs eventually subsided. I saw a light at the end of the alcohol tunnel. Today, I am not an alcoholic. I am not even a recovering alcoholic. I am just a man who does not have any thoughts about life's challenges anymore. I am simply me. We are not the labels the world has made. Stopping thoughts and finding peace within allows us to see that we are free and whole and always were. It is the ego that describes us as insufficient. I now know something about the mind that I would have never known had I not battled alcohol and come out the other side. For that, I am grateful.

So, as a sober guy I decided to track down this blissful feeling without the help of drugs or alcohol. For a few years, I managed to redirect my thoughts by bombarding my mind with positive messages, but now I needed to know how to stop thinking altogether. I realized, purely by accident, that extreme sports would stop thought. When riding a motorcycle at breakneck speeds, it is challenging to think. You have to instinctively "do." There is no time for thoughts. Thoughts about making motorcycle payments are not going to keep me alive at high speeds. There is only enough time to be completely dialed into oneness with the bike.

This was an epiphany to me because it gave me a glimpse into "no thought," all while being sober. Bliss really is attainable. This must be how workaholics feel, so tuned into work that passing thoughts never creep in. Turns out, this no thought thing can be found any time a person is dialed into this creative mode. Artists can be so caught up in their work that they forget what time it is or that they have not eaten. Time stands still. Even with this knowledge, I was unable to attain a place of no thought, but I was not ready to give up.

I decided to use a stopwatch to help me while sitting still. I would set the timer for two minutes. I would politely ask any passing thought to leave as I returned to no thought. This worked, but it was sloppy, and progress was slow. I heard about the body being an anchor for the mind to achieve no thought. The mind's uncontrollable need to be solving a problem or looking out for your well-being runs on autopilot. I knew I could stop the thoughts by multitasking the mind.

The basic idea is to ask the mind to think about the five senses of the body, to purposefully notice the breath going in and going out. Notice the chest rising and falling. Notice the way the chair feels on your back. Notice the smells, the sounds. All of this sensual perception is awareness, but with no labels of right or wrong. No matter the sound, even if it is an annoying dog barking, allow it, and be aware of it, but without a judgment or label. This trains the mind to pay attention. The mind will constantly interrupt this process at first. It will tell you to check and see if the stove is turned off or tell you this practice is stupid, but if you stick with it, it works.

Despite the mind's attempt to take back control, remind the mind that you are using only two quick minutes. This is not suppression of emotions, nor is this avoidance. It is just stating a fact - just two minutes. This will calm the mind enough to get a glimpse, if only for a few seconds, of nirvana in the middle of a very chaotic world. I have experienced bliss. I have learned to utilize these two minutes of no thought during different parts of my day. The key is to ask your mind to be still without the pressure of success and no feelings of guilt if you make absolutely no progress. The idea is to simply start a new habit by taking two minutes for yourself. When a person is on vacation and feeling good, the mind is relaxed. Is this suppression of emotions even though there are still bills to pay? Of course not. Did all your problems need to be solved before taking a vacation so that you could feel good? Of course not. Taking two minutes to excuse thoughts purposefully and gently from this two-minute session is more valuable to your health than a vacation because it becomes a tool that can be used to align the mind to the peace that passes all understanding even during the most stressful events or in the middle of the night when the mind is racing.

I began to get better at this, and I incorporated this into my nightly bedtime routine. I used to suffer from insomnia. As a youngster, I would drink alcohol to help me sleep. I remember my mother discovering beer bottles in my bedroom at sixteen or seventeen years old. At the age of fifty, I finally know what it is like to sleep a full night and I must say it has been a game changer in my mental health. I used to have trouble falling asleep because of my worries. I would wake in the middle of the night with a racing mind that worried about everything from the inane to the important.

If I awoke during the night, I learned how to turn my thoughts to my breathing. My mind had taken control of my life in such a destructive way and once again, I felt like a prisoner peering out from behind the metal bars of my cell. In the same way that I had the key to my recovery from alcohol, I also held the key to my battle with insomnia. I used to get up in the middle of the night, tackle the worries of my mind, and climb back into bed hoping for a little shuteye. Now, instead of calming the mind through completing these insane 2 am tasks, I place my mind on the five senses of the body and drift peacefully asleep. Not every night is a complete success, but most nights I fall asleep with a childlike anticipation for the next day and dream of the previous day's blessings.

Chapter Six

THE WORLD IS A DREAM

Most people are living from their false self but are doing so subconsciously. There are two reasons for this. The first being they have forgotten that they are the spirit. Entering the physical world through their mother's womb is much like entering the dream phase of sleep. When we drift off to sleep at night, we may find ourselves playing the starring role in a movie in our mind without even knowing how we got there. Entering this world though the womb is similar. There is no recollection of who we truly are. Our birthday suit is nothing like the spirit of awareness that peers out through the eyes of the body. We see the body, the world of physical forms, and begin to relate to the physical dimension from the limited and finite view of the mind.

Dreams can be intensely felt, much like our physical lives. Entering this physical world through the womb leaves not a trace of evidence of the spirit life from which we came. There is a realm, portal, or dimension, whichever term you prefer, that gives us a glimpse into this truth. This place is the stillness of no thought. You are able to travel here when the false self is removed. It is through this awareness that you will understand the physical world you currently live in is nearly the same as the dream-like state of mind we enter while sleeping.

The second reason people choose to live from the false self is because it feels good to the ego. There is a difference between the egoic feelings and the feelings of the true spirit. Egoic feelings are tied to worldly events and to a person's thoughts. These feelings of joy or sadness are felt as we ride the roller coaster of life. The wins and losses are felt much like the "reality" of dreams are felt as you sleep. Over time, this illusion of worldly highs and lows is made known by the unanswered questions and inner voids that seem endless.

When living life from the true self, the wins and losses are seen in much the same way as how dreams are remembered upon waking. The dream is seen as something separate and not real even though during the dream you may have been sweating or breathing heavily. When you are aligned with no thought, you are able to awake from the world as if it were a dream (which it actually is) but while you are still physically in the world (which is actually a dream or illusion).

Also in our dream world is the illusion of others. This is a bit strange but if you put into practice what I am about to tell you from a true mental place of alignment, life will be more accommodating. Every person and situation in the world is here to help you become more deeply aligned. Let's talk about some of the things that might be easier to grasp. The first are people. From the kid down the street to the angry clerk, they are reflecting back to you, yourself. Exclude the physical dimension while thinking about this. Whatever emotional state of expression you are receiving from the people you encounter is a chance for you to go deeper into alignment or go around the same emotional mountain again.

The young kid on the side of the road with a broken bike is a reflection of you. Again, stay in the emotional realm. He is in need and is too shy to ask. If you meet his emotional needs, that is to say, you help him from a state of alignment, you have helped yourself. If you help him to show how great you are to your friends, you have missed the mark. This type of living requires a person to be real. That is, real about your emotions. When you become emotionally vulnerable and help another from a place of love, you have loved yourself. If you help from an egoic place of needing approval from others, you have expanded the negative vibration of the world.

Outside of staying aligned, nothing else matters. When you align, you let life flow through you. Staying aligned requires a true commitment to the integrity and love of self. By doing so, you single-handedly help the world. When you meet the angry clerk and you drop resistance, become emotionally transparent, and allow the clerk to be angry, you have shined the eternal light of divinity. You will not contribute to the negativity of the world. There is a difference between allowing the clerk to be angry, while you ignore your own inner emotions of disgust by pretending it is okay with you and being aligned. When you are aligned, the negativity and anger has nowhere to spread. By ignoring the emotion in you and pretending you are okay with it, or worse, retaliating, you have moved the needle of worldly negative vibrations another notch in the wrong direction.

That angry clerk's emotions (not the clerk himself) are the reflection of what is inside of you. Treat the emotions with love through alignment and you have furthered the vibration of love in the world. This is not suppression of emotions or misdirecting emotions. This is seeing the emotions in another and being the light. It requires you to become transparent and allow the emotions of another to pass right through you. Most of us resist angry emotions from others. We put our walls up and this preserves anger inside us.

Being emotionally vulnerable is only a part of the story. When aligned, you are being emotionally powerful. Other people appear threatening when we are under the influence of the ego. When we see past the egoic, false self in another by being connected to Source Energy, we join hands from one expression of Consciousness to another. In doing so, negative energy is dissolved. This can also have a divine effect on the individual expressing anger. It is entirely possible for that individual's negative energy to leave them. They may feel better after having spoken to you and not even know why.

Most times when we emotionally help another it is not our specific words or actions that have made an impact. Words and actions are wonderful ways of expressing love, empathy, and compassion, but bringing a new vibrational tone of peaceful energy is the real reason they might feel better.

Chapter Seven

BLACK SKY

Why do people verbalize elevated emotions? When you articulate that you are too excited or too nervous to sleep, you are expressing these feelings from an emotional foundation devoid of alignment. When aligned, emotions do not escalate outside of a tolerance of internal harmony. Happiness, sadness, joy, excitement, and so forth are experienced but are felt within the constraints of good mental health. Emotions are not given unrestricted permission to rob our good mental or physical health. Without alignment, you allow your emotions to take over.

You may feel out of control. Overeating, insomnia, excessive drinking, anxiety, and so forth appear as outward signs that a person has traded good health for an erroneous thought. That thought comes in the form of misalignment to the physical world rather than aligning to your pure essence. Feeling like you are out of control steals your sense of peace, but more importantly this form of thought appears to you as something you have no control over. You search the world of physical form for a physical remedy for relief.

Pills, therapy, and so forth bring only an impermanent relief. You may be temporarily patched up with a superficial treatment. Why? Because the negative energy in the body is formed from the non-physical. A permanent solution in the form of pills or therapy does not appear to exist as the world's suffering increases year after year. These solutions do not exist in the physical places where you might search. Many solutions, created in the physical realm, such as pills or therapy can sometimes prevent a person from feeling emotions instead of giving someone the tools to temper emotional responses to acceptable levels.

In essence, the emotional levels run rampant because there is no deep level of alignment to Source Energy. Alignment to Source in itself does not control or restrict emotions. Alignment, in a sense, gives a person license to be who they are divinely meant to be. This unrestricted element is the key to a person's freedom from suffering. When you live from an inner place of abundance at all times, you have no restrictions. If you live from the false self, you live 90% of your life in a restricted and guarded mode. This steals energy as it whispers "protection" to the individual.

With the restricted, false self comes a need to purge stored energy. This comes in the form of so much excitement or anxiety that it causes a disruption in your sleep. The stored-up energy is what would normally be considered a healthy energy. It is the energy of the higher and creative self. Humans inadvertently restrict the ebb and flow of the natural release of this energy. When we live aligned, our energy flow is unrestricted, abundant, natural, and easy.

Following the internal signals that come with alignment for the entirety of the day allows energy to flow unrestricted. Peace and a sense that time is standing still will arise in your life through alignment. Unfortunately, the egoic, false self shouts louder than the harmonic voice of Source Energy and many will revert back to their old habitual patterns. They are tricked into trusting more in the egoic voice of distrust and uneasiness than in the voice of Source. Why? Because this voice of distrust plays on human fears. Without alignment to our divine nature, we see our physical form and trust the physical thoughts of insufficiency.

Making the leap from being mentally anchored in the physical realm to being anchored in the divine realm is the hardest part. The thinking mind only perceives the physical realm from which it is based. People use this thinking mind as if it is the Holy Grail. It is not. When not aligned, the thinking mind is just as much an illusion as the chair you are sitting on. The chair is 99.9% moving energy and therefore the entity you see is an illusion. Thoughts from the foundation of the false self are an illusion. To place trust in your anxiety is like thinking the chair is not moving energy.

Yes, you feel the realness of anxiety as it cripples you and your life. That is completely true, but once you make the mental leap into the realm of alignment, you realize a new truth. For the longest time we thought the earth was flat or the sky was truly blue. There are tons of these moments of discovery. What happened after the discovery is more important than the discovery itself. Once you are made aware of something that you never knew existed, you are able to advance confidently in a new direction. A mental shift happens, and a new truth opens up.

There is a realm of peace that belongs to you. You do not need the physical world to do anything. You do not need security, love, or anything else from the physical world. You just think you need it. You think you need something so much so that you are subconsciously choosing to suffer until it is physically manifested. The epiphany comes when you realize all of the things you think you desperately need are already abundant within you. We used to think the sky was blue. We discovered outer space and realized there is actually blackness above our heads. Humans see blue but not because it is really blue. There is another scientific reason we see blue, but I will let you Google that.

The epiphany comes when you realize that your hard-core truth is not really valid. The blue sky is not really blue but appears so. The same can be said for the physical forms, our thoughts developed from the false self, and the things we think we are missing, like security, love, and so forth. They also appear to be just like that blue sky. They seem real, but why? The answer is simple, we just did not know the truth. Once we know that we are truly abundantly blessed beyond our imagination, we do not fall for the "blue sky" tricks of the physical form anymore.

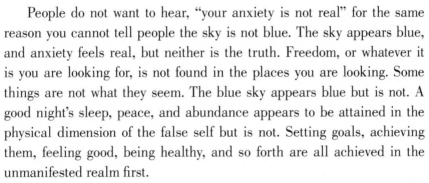

Chapter Eight
FOOD FOR THOUGHT

People do not want to hear, "your anxiety is not real" for the same reason you cannot tell people the sky is not blue. The sky appears blue, and anxiety feels real, but neither is the truth. Freedom, or whatever it is you are looking for, is not found in the places you are looking. Some things are not what they seem. The blue sky appears blue but is not. A good night's sleep, peace, and abundance appears to be attained in the physical dimension of the false self but is not. Setting goals, achieving them, feeling good, being healthy, and so forth are all achieved in the unmanifested realm first.

Anxiety seems to be a persistent and endless challenge. The mind will continually throw fastballs in the form of thoughts at you. Do this. Worry about that. What should I have said? What should I say later? It is never ending and extremely tiresome. Practicing no thought during the good times is the key to hitting the fastball out of the park. Practicing this every moment you are able allows you to rewire your brain and break away from the old habitual patterns. It takes mental work. It is exhausting but well worth it.

Does anyone know what their purpose on earth is? Is everyone behaving in ways dictated by the ego? Is anxiety your obligation to carry through life? Is some form of worldly accomplishment your obligation?

Who are you? Are you the guy or gal that made the grade? Failed the test? Was promoted or fired? One way to tell if you are being run by the ego is if you cannot seem to catch a break. Are you thinking anything outside of alignment?

The ego is starving for attention. The ego needs you to look at someone else, compare yourself, and contend that the other person is awful. In order for the ego to stay alive, it needs you to compare. The ego hates it when you sit alone in no thought. It needs you to get up and eat even though you are not hungry. The ego needs you to make disparaging remarks about others. Are you bored sitting still in no thought? Is your mind metaphorically tapping its toes, waiting for this nonsense of no thought to end so you can get on to more important things?

What is more important than enjoying life, right as it is, at this very moment? Has the ego ever let you rest? Are you where you want to be in life? Are you the right weight or the right size? Do you have the right job? Are things, people, and situations still bothering you? How long has this been going on? Has the ego ever gotten you to a permanent destination, to a perfect partner, or perfect financial status? What is the one common denominator? Are you still waiting for something? Again, how long have you been struggling, striving, waiting in misery?

Do you feel the pull from the ego to start doing something other than no thought? Why do you still believe that your mind/the ego/your thoughts, will eventually take you to a place of rest, reward, and peace? Is anxiety keeping you on edge? Are you tired of covering it up and pretending like all is well? Would you like to finally have what the ego has never delivered to you? Will you get fed up enough to take a stand or will you eventually die trying everything the misinformed ego tells you to try?

Did you know that a piece of you will die when you say no to the ego? Is that what is holding you back? Fear not. It is the scared part inside of you that will die. When you finally stop listening to the voice inside your head, you realize your security blanket will perish. That security blanket has not been your friend. You continue to rely on your egoic, false self even when promises have gone unfulfilled for ten, twenty, or even fifty years

Your false self has been stroking your hair, telling you that it will be okay. It holds a straw to your mouth, and you willingly taste the sweetness of its poison. Your anxiety, depression, and fear are the by-product of its destruction. It tells you it is on your side, helping you. It whispers for you to stay in your head thinking about nothing and everything all at the same time.

Are you fed up with the reverberations of the egoic mind? Have you had enough anxiety, depression, and pain? Do you want relief? The answer is not outside of you. Let the ego die. Stop listening to it. You are not depressed, anxious, or fearful. You just have been told to think so. Do you want to sleep like a baby tonight? Do you want to feel like you have a purpose? Would you like to stop feeling like you have the weight of the world bearing down on your tired soul? Would you like to feel free?

Ask yourself why the egoic voice in your head does not want you to practice no thought for two minutes. Go ahead. Ask. Take an account of how many days it has been since you had peace of mind. Did you feel the peace that passes all understanding yesterday? The day before? No time? Had to work? Had to take care of the kids? No time to practice two minutes of self-loving peace? Are you sure "you" said you do not have the time? Maybe there is an egoic voice in your head steering from your subconscious? Possibly?

Give it two minutes. Two minutes and you may begin to notice the deeper you that senses some truth in this theory? Can you feel its presence inside your body and mind? It has no voice. It is just there. It is waiting for you to acknowledge it. It is your higher self. It has been waiting for you all along, waiting for you to wake up from this nightmare.

Chapter Nine

ENERGY DEPLETION

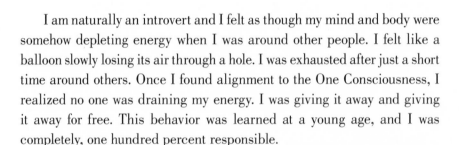

I am naturally an introvert and I felt as though my mind and body were somehow depleting energy when I was around other people. I felt like a balloon slowly losing its air through a hole. I was exhausted after just a short time around others. Once I found alignment to the One Consciousness, I realized no one was draining my energy. I was giving it away and giving it away for free. This behavior was learned at a young age, and I was completely, one hundred percent responsible.

Why I did this at such a young age is less important than *how* I fixed this dilemma as an adult. While living my life through alignment, the primary importance is alignment itself. Figuring out the why will come later. Through the act of alignment, I recognized this depletion of energy came from me. Once aligned, all things will feel harmonious to the spirit, and at the same time, may feel awful to the false, egoic self which dissolves with time.

In my case, I blamed others for this energy depletion. I referred to myself as an introvert through an act of stroking the ego and denying the spirit. At a young age, many of us learn to deny the spirit and feed the ego. This misalignment will likely be the cause of some of the body's systems to eventually malfunction. For me, insomnia and digestive issues were a result. Lack of alignment caused an incredible amount of stress in my body.

Living through the false self distorts what is actually happening. I blamed others for this energy depletion, and I truly thought it to be real. Perception is reality, after all. As you peer through the eyes of the false self, a completely incorrect world view is realized. It is only through alignment that you can see the truth and eventually recognize the way in which your view of life has been distorted.

Once aligned, you recognize that you, and you alone, are at fault. You are singly responsible for your own life. The energy of your sizable ego and its formidable threats begin to change. The ego evaporates almost into thin air as this new energy is felt. This new energy is called the peace that passes all understanding. The label of introvert for myself still exists in many ways, but I do not give away my energy anymore. Other people do not deplete my energy. They cannot. I recognize who I am through alignment. Through the daily practice of alignment, I began to slowly release the chains that bound me. I was motivated by the small glimpse of peace that came from just minutes of stillness. With more practice, I began to extend the period of no thought from minutes to days.

An unaligned introvert will become depleted when around others, but it is not others who are taking away energy. A deep-rooted, mental state of peace should always be the foundation of the aligned person. Even through difficult scenarios, you will feel the peace that passes all understanding. It is still possible to be at peace while dealing with difficult scenarios. Being at peace is not defined simply as being in a mental place of happiness. It is entirely possible to be at peace and to be unhappy at the same time.

While aligned as an introvert, I am at peace in the company of others, and I do not give away any of my energy - for free or otherwise. It is impossible to deplete my own energy or let others take away my energy when I am aligned. This realization becomes clear once alignment is reached. There are two reasons this truth might escape you. The first is a belief in the egoic, false self. This belief is so deep, you will suffer right down to the moment of your death. That is how strongly one might hold on to the lie that comes with the ego. The second reason many are unable to know the truth through alignment is because getting to this place of stillness requires absolutely nothing from you. That bears repeating, alignment requires **nothing from you.**

Many can understand the first reason mentioned. You may recognize that there is an egoic deception taking place. I actually think it can be felt while not aligned. Years of suffering does seem to make you ask important questions, even those living from the lies of the ego. The second reason I mentioned will likely be the most difficult to comprehend. Even though we can see that the tree in nature does "nothing" as it harmoniously contributes to the world in the form of providing beauty, cleaning the air we breathe, giving home to animals, and so on, we find it terribly difficult to make that assumption about ourselves. That is to say that we can do "nothing," just like the tree, and still make great contributions to the world while simultaneously getting our bills paid and the children off to school.

In biblical times, it may have appeared easier for an individual to trust in God or Source Energy, to supply his/her basic needs. Without modern conveniences, it may have been easier for people to rely on God for food, water, and shelter. Somehow, that is easier for us to understand. Even today, we believe that God could surely supply a person, roaming the desert, with a source of water, food, and materials to build a house. However, those same people do not feel that God will certainly provide a means to pay the bills in today's busy world. Life seems to get in the way. Work, modern technology, and deadlines are critical tasks that are not seen as something you could "do nothing" about. Trees can do nothing, but it seems that people must work.

Those same people facing threats felt just as some of us do today. How can God supply my needs? God cannot search the internet for a job for me. Maybe a long time ago a person roaming the desert could trust God for a source of water and food, but surely God does not know how to reset my pin number so I can pay the mortgage online. In reality, those people did not find it easy to trust that God will keep them safe from the hungry lion. Your needs will be provided when you align. Your needs change when aligned. There is no longer a need for the physical world to satisfy you. Once a glimpse of alignment is attained, a desire to become aligned for longer periods of time occurs. Eventually the desire to be aligned is no more. Alignment and internal peace become a way of life.

The difference in responsibilities from caveman times to present day is very extreme and therefore, you may find it difficult to rely on God to get the bills paid. This is exactly how it is seen through the false self. When aligned, it is entirely possible to leave the stress behind, stay at peace, *and* get the bills paid. It is not only possible, but any other way seems like insanity to the one who is aligned. For me, I seem to be able to live from both places. I still need to make a conscious choice to stay aligned and therefore, still keep both perspectives.

This is one of the reasons I am writing this book. During my awakening, I felt drawn to communicate this process of enlightenment. The deeper I dove into the process, the more I felt a pull to leave the false self entirely, never to return. I have felt a calling to write about my experience so that others might be able to make a conscious choice to be in a place of peace rather than to be wrestled into peace because of intense suffering, like I was. It does not need to be that challenging. Through alignment, even insignificant topics, such as the energy-draining moments of an introvert, are explained and overcome. Overcome is not really the right word. It is more like a shift or change of power. The false self is seen as a layer that interferes with being at peace.

At some point, I felt called to follow the inner promptings of my heart and record my journey. This is my attempt to do "nothing" just like the tree. While on this journey of doing nothing (which is how the ego may see my efforts) my physical body feels the best it has ever felt. My digestive track finally functions properly after years of discomfort. Decades of insomnia are followed by good sleeping patterns. Bad habits disappeared all on their own with absolutely no effort on my part. Good habits were picked up and embraced. Suicidal depression, anxiety, and other negative emotions vanished into thin air.

Alignment does require you to leave your old ways and habits behind, but it will happen. This can be scary to the ego. Your career, friends, etcetera may change, and change can be hard as seen from the false self. The egoic voice of fear of the unknown will speak. Our choice and freewill is to suffer right into submission or take the gift of peace. I decided to give this a try. I decided to do nothing, as the ego would call it. Out of me, will surface something unique and special. A contribution to the world that will be just as much "nothing" as the tree's contribution to the earth.

Hopefully, at some point, you will choose peace over suffering. Make it a conscious choice - through alignment. If the methods in this book do not resonate with you, find your own path. Signs that you are on the right path will be that your mind and body feel good. Emotions can lead the way, not through egoic pleasures that feed the inner void, but by emotions that feed the spirit. You will know when it is right because you will not have to ask if you are on the correct path anymore. In my case, I utilized my body as a signal for being on the right path or not. As I listen to how my body feels, I am guided towards the right path. I was diagnosed with osteoarthritis. This pain went away with alignment. I know I am either thinking or doing something not in accordance with my baseline when the small signals of discomfort arise within my body.

Chapter Ten

CHANGE YOUR THOUGHTS, CHANGE THE WORLD

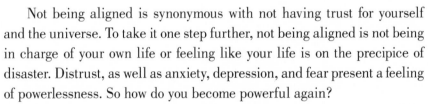

Not being aligned is synonymous with not having trust for yourself and the universe. To take it one step further, not being aligned is not being in charge of your own life or feeling like your life is on the precipice of disaster. Distrust, as well as anxiety, depression, and fear present a feeling of powerlessness. So how do you become powerful again?

The world is a three-dimensional image of ourselves. Our view of the world reflects our individual thoughts, images, paradigms, and conditioning. It is important to remember that your view of the world will be different from someone else's. This is a key truth to being able to understand your own particular life because it points to the fact that your thoughts, however distorted or true, will signal to the world to reverberate the same.

When you change the way you think, you change the world. It really is that simple, but because most people are so set in believing their thoughts, they point to the world as the source of their problems. If you are willing to test the theory, start making small mental shifts in thinking and see if the world reflects back to you the same. Loving thoughts created from a deeply rooted and hidden place of distrust and lack will produce more distrust and lack even if you are outwardly projecting forms of love. That is why alignment is important. When aligned, the individual and unique expression of Consciousness will align with the One Consciousness. This is where the false self and those deeply rooted hidden places of distrust and lack will be revealed. At that point, your inner vibration and the One Consciousness' vibration are the same. All truth, harmony, and peace exist there. Through this inner shift is where true outer change is made.

Chapter Eleven

INSIDE AN ANXIOUS MIND

———————————⟶⟿———————————

Hopefully, you do not know what the inside of a mind with chronic anxiety looks like. This is how I used to perceive the world before I knew what alignment was.

It is five am. I slumped out of bed after sleeping for about two hours. It has been over three weeks since I have slept more than two hours or woke up feeling refreshed. My body aches as I debate whether I will kill myself today or I will pretend to be happy. Both options are equally horrifying. I prepare myself for a day of pretending to care about the same dull things everyone else seems to care about. Unbeknownst to me, some do not have uncontrollable emotions of fear. I figured everyone else must be insane because no one seems to address the tormenting mind. I guess they all just ignore it, so I will try to as well.

This fear is not really fear as the average person might know it. It is not the average definition of being afraid. Others are afraid they might look foolish if their friends notice the large, red pimple just under their nose. The fear I am talking about is dark, too mentally heavy to lift, and certainly too horrifying to mentally look at. Its threats come laced with pain unlike any physical pain I have ever known. Once I sawed through the young, thin skin on my left wrist with a brown-handled, serrated, 1980's-style kitchen knife. Just under the area where a watch band might rest, the knife broke through the skin. Every tiny curvature of the serrated edge grabbed the tendon on my wrist. Even the physical pain of the dull kitchen knife was nothing compared to the mental anguish that pressed into the depths of my mind.

Life went on like this for many, many years. As an adult, I learned to hide the mental pain from myself and others. Life appeared to get better as I learned to self-medicate and treat the effects of anxiety. I learned coping mechanisms that never went to the root of the problem like alignment does. I would learn how to function as an adult with anxiety, never knowing there was a way to get rid of anxiety. Distraction and redirection became ways of life to cope with the rising levels of unease and mental stress. Over exercising, overeating, drinking, excessive complaining, judging, and just about anything that would take me away from my current thoughts became a coping mechanism for me.

It was not until alignment occurred in my life that I was able to view anxiety as separate from me. I was able to see anxiety like looking at a broken arm or a cut in the skin. After alignment, I was able to disconnect from its grips. That in itself did not solve anything, but it enabled me to see that the methods of relief I had been utilizing were, in fact, coping mechanisms that treated the symptoms, and not the root cause.

After I disconnected from anxiety, I needed to "sit" with it as it was. This second phase helped me to further dis-identify with it as well as establish that anxiety, in it of itself, cannot hurt me. Furthermore, sitting with it as a separate entity allowed me to see what was truly hurting me, which was my thoughts about it. The steps I took slowly reduced the power of the negative energy and gave the power back to me. I was finally working on the root cause of my anxiety.

The work was not finished though. Even though I now knew the truth, I was not free and clear. Even though I sat with this negative energy, I had not actually looked at it. During one night of sitting with the negative energy of insomnia (i.e., not allowing it to overtake me with fear and staying in a mental state of peace) I decided to look at it. When I did, it disappeared. This proved my theory that negative energy is a fictitious monster hiding under a child's bed. It is not real. It just feels real. It feels so real that I could not even bear to look at it.

After all this, I was still not completely rid of anxiety, and other negative emotions. I would continue to have moments where panic attacks would pop up out of nowhere. I think this was due to habitual brain patterns, but simply repeating the steps above would dissolve all of its energy. I no longer feel negative energy for more than just a second, and if it occurs, it is now seen as a signal that I have lost my connection and alignment. Very few times does that happen anymore.

Chapter Twelve

EVICTING ANXIETY

———————

For years, I suffered from chronic, debilitating anxiety. I started drinking at an early age as a way to lull my brain to sleep. I was never able to turn off my overactive mind, so I looked to alcohol for relief. When this no longer worked, I found extreme sports to be an effective way to disengage from the anxiety. Riding a motorcycle at high speeds did not allow for anxious thoughts about the past or future. In fact, the suicidal depression I suffered seemed to encourage dangerous sports, as I did not seem to care about life.

I did not know it at the time, but anxiety was a way of life for me. Anxiety is rooted in fear, while the opposite of fear is trust. Simply put, anxiety is a lack of trust, but lack of trust in what? This question lingered and is what propelled me forward on my journey to pursue the truth.

For me, anxiety was formed from a subconscious coping mechanism I developed as a kid. I was frightened of school and of my peers. I was bullied as a child, and as a result, I was unable to develop meaningful relationships with schoolmates. With no real tools for coping, I subconsciously turned on the fight-or-flight mode to keep me safe. On Sunday nights, this dysfunctional method of coping would begin and finally, on Friday, it would end. What should have been a safe haven for learning, quickly became a terrifying place of unrest - meeting my bullies regularly Monday through Friday at school. And so it was, for the next thirty-nine years, I lived with a subconscious mental pattern that habitually ran on repeat in the background of my mind.

As a child, I envisioned Monday to be the color black. Monday was the first day of school and when the bullying would begin. I color-coded Fridays as green. To me, green signified peace as the upcoming weekend, without the difficulties of school, was approaching. Gradually, the time frame of mental peace and the color green, would diminish over the weekend. In anticipation of Monday, I began to experience anxiety and these horrible, fearful emotions, earlier and earlier in the weekend. Eventually, my peaceful mental state of mind only lasted a few short hours on Saturday. Unfortunately, I carried this throughout most of my adult life.

I became aware of this habitual pattern completely by accident. On a long, eight-hour drive home from Vermont, I listened to some self-help audio stuff on the radio. Oddly, I noticed that my normal levels of anxiety had subsided upon my return home. My "normal" was to feel anxiety all week long, Monday through Friday, just like when I was a child in school. I never knew why until now. So, after noticing that distracting my mind with positive audio for eight hours straight could rewire my brain, albeit ever so slightly, I began to do this intentionally over the next five years.

It dawned on me that I no longer associated fear (and the color black) with *any* day of the week. This was quite a profound realization, and an enormous amount of gratitude enveloped me. There is no substitute for mental peace - none. I have truly found peace within. No worldly event or material object could replace the wonderful feeling of peace within.

I suppose I finally changed who I began listening to in my head. Switching the mental authority figures in your mind is a big hurdle to overcome before you can get to a peaceful state of being. Ever present is the little voice inside your head constantly telling you what to do. It keeps you awake at night complaining, labeling, and judging. It compares you to others, stirs up emotions of guilt or pride, and you believe in it wholeheartedly. The other authority figure is the combination of the "you" as the emanation of the One Consciousness and the One Consciousness.

The "you," as the emanation of the One Consciousness, is not your name, history, job title, etcetera. This is the "you" that is the divine essence. It is the "you" peering through human eyes, noticing the world from a place of peace. If you do not know inner peace from a place of security, love, and abundance, you may not know who "you" truly are. This "you" is found inside the still and present mind. When this "you," as an emanation of the One Consciousness, is combined with the One Consciousness, "you" are under the influence of Source Energy.

When aligned, the mental voice that keeps you awake at night, is realized for what it is. It is a habitual pattern of thought that you unwittingly let run your life straight into fear. It becomes so deeply ingrained inside that you completely identify with it as you. Dethroning this illusion is perhaps the biggest hurdle because you see it as you. You must gather all of your trust and place it somewhere else. Rather than allowing this pattern of thought to run your life, you will have to let no thought run your life.

At first, I distracted my mind, and did so often, but without the dedication I later became determined to have. Once I started noticing larger improvements in how I felt, I became intensely involved in my recovery efforts. Somewhere in 2020, I dedicated my life to being a guinea pig of sorts for this personal experiment. I had nothing to lose. I had already "failed" at life through living by my own conditioning and paradigms. I did not want to go around the same mountain again. I also came to the sad realization of just how many people I hurt by living from a place of fear.

I take full responsibility for my circumstances in life, but with zero guilt. It was a journey of learning. As a person fully committed to aligning with Source at every moment, I am content. With that disclaimer out of the way, I would like to talk to you about how our lives directly reflect what is on the *inside* of us. Our lives do not always mirror the physical energy we use when we look for something we feel might be missing. Our lives reflect the place from which you broadcast your spiritual signal.

I used to transmit my signal from fear. Even though I sent the physical message to the world that I was unafraid by riding motorcycles, jumping from airplanes, rock climbing, and so on, my basis for life was built on fear. I did not truly know this at the time. This is a critical point to understand. I was working so hard to attain love and trust through worldly action and yet the world never reciprocated. Why? Because I sent the message while I was not aligned with Source Energy.

We become detached from Source Energy for many reasons. As I stated earlier, I detached, through no fault of my own, as a child trying to protect myself. Consequently, throughout life I stood on a foundation of fear that promised to protect me from bullies and so forth. It worked, but it also kept me from alignment, healthy friendships, peace and most importantly, trust. As I lived my life, I was outwardly struggling and striving to be on the outside what I hated on the inside. I struggled to be free and trusting of the world, but I did so on the worldly plain. This type of "efforting" is the equivalent to running a brush down a mirror and wondering why your hair is still messed up.

I later learned that alignment with Source Energy is all we really need. I also learned that most people, due to their low level of discomfort in the form of boredom, depression, anxiety, and so forth, do things in an attempt to steer clear of negative emotions. In other words, people like myself, live life completely opposite of how their subconscious feels in an effort to overcome the low-level, negative emotions of separation from Source. This "efforting" appears to be natural, but in fact it is dysfunctional and is camouflaged from most who do it. Obviously, not all of us are doing this, but many do.

This is the illusion. We think we need material possessions to make us happy, but these things are given to us once we are fulfilled on the inside. This is alignment. This is terribly difficult to wrap the mind around because humans are firm believers in Newtonian-type laws in the physical realm. We believe so much in the illusion of our so-called reality that we think the only way to happiness is to place the comb on the mirror to brush our hair. We truly want to make lasting change, but it cannot be manifested in the real world, with any type of permanency or true peace, by means of "effort" without alignment. Worldly change that is full of peace, love, and trust, only comes to those who broadcast their signal while joining hands with Source Energy. Any other platform from which the signal is dispatched will reflect back with lack and insufficiency.

Anxiety is shown the door when we realize this. It just takes awareness to make anxiety dissolve. This did not happen overnight for me. In fact, I acknowledged small moments in time of self-awareness. Eventually, entire days would pass by without a panic attack. This was huge for me. Panic attacks came for no reason at all. There was no outward reason for it in my adult life and yet there it was, rearing its ugly head. I would feel fear, break out in sweat, and experience an enormous weight compressing my entire body.

It was through awareness that I set myself free. I stopped believing in it so much. I allowed it to rise up in me and I somehow watched it from afar, like an out-of-body experience. I acknowledged it and it quickly dissipated. I later realized what I was witnessing was this habitual reaction in my body from the safety of alignment with Source.

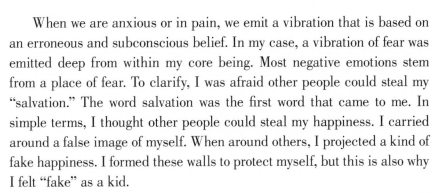

Chapter Thirteen
VIBRATIONAL PULL

When we are anxious or in pain, we emit a vibration that is based on an erroneous and subconscious belief. In my case, a vibration of fear was emitted deep from within my core being. Most negative emotions stem from a place of fear. To clarify, I was afraid other people could steal my "salvation." The word salvation was the first word that came to me. In simple terms, I thought other people could steal my happiness. I carried around a false image of myself. When around others, I projected a kind of fake happiness. I formed these walls to protect myself, but this is also why I felt "fake" as a kid.

This was a mental construct I formed when young to protect myself from bullies. Even though I was whole, healed, abundant, and blessed, I placed more precedence on what the bullies thought of me than what my true divine nature was. In a subconscious attempt to cover up what appeared to be disliked by others in me, I put on a "false self." This identity was a child's way of protection. I was identifying with a false image of myself and considering it to be true.

If we substitute the word salvation for happiness, or maybe inner peace, it might make more sense. You may look for salvation, happiness, or inner peace in others. I thought others could take away my inner peace. In some cases, we may feel that others give us inner peace. This revelation brought me even farther from the false self. I realized the anxiety I felt as an adult, during Zoom calls and other public speaking events, was because I thought that all those people could take away my inner peace or that they could see something awful inside of me, similar to what I thought the bullies saw in me.

Not knowing your spiritual "roots" is a quick way to get lost in this world. Through the practice of alignment, you know who you truly are and the subconscious vibrations stemming from fear, lack, and insufficiency, are quickly dispelled. The other important part to this is the fact that there is an effort to cover up a vibration of insufficiency that does not exist. This is fundamental. On the deepest level, you are whole, healed, worthy, accepted, approved, and abundant. The reason you may not feel this way could be because you are listening to the inner voice of the false self.

Sometimes we are covering up something. Sometimes we are covering up something that does not exist. The only way to know if it truly exists within you is to look directly at it with a sense of love through the act of alignment. If anxiety, depression, and other negative emotions are still a part of your life, you may not be looking directly at it. You may think you are, but if you do not know your divine spiritual roots, you will fall for the lies of the ego.

A heavy burden is carried by people who solely identify with their false self. This burden is the egoic illusion of their human weakness. They try to conceal it by focusing on their egoic strengths. In some ways, the attempt to cover up the weakness is like a child covering their eyes and saying, "If I can't see you, you can't see me." Like this analogy, they are not hiding their weaknesses from others. Instead, they do not realize they are trying to hide the weakness from themselves.

When aligned, the burden carried is light. It is light because it is only the egoic "idea" of who you thought you were. Once this is acknowledged, even that burden disappears. All that is left is to be the light.

The enemy, negative emotions, and so on, only exist because we created it. Through love and alignment peace is found. This peace is the wonderful mental state of mind we get to traverse life with. We have been deceived into believing we are lacking because of the strong pull of the physical world and its relationship to our own physical body. In order to know the relationship between your own divine essence and the creator of the universe, one must transcend the thinking mind through alignment and no thought.

With alignment comes a certain wisdom that can be felt vibrationally. I followed my inner pull to move to the western part of the United States to be closer to my two children. After I moved, I felt another vibrational calling. I am writing this book in real-time with my life. I do not know whether what I am about to describe will pan out or not. I do know that I have not stopped following the guidance from the inner wisdom that arises from alignment. Only time will tell if I took the right action or not. I am also aware that the right action is in the eye of the beholder.

My thoughts were to move to Las Vegas and land a second job. I figured I would work my tail to the bone, as I have always done, to get the mortgage paid off quickly. I applied for multiple jobs and went on several interviews. I was qualified for each job and in every circumstance, I was told I would be hired. In the end, I did not accept any of the jobs and here is the reason why. Through alignment, I was steered away. Perhaps a better explanation was that I was steered *towards* something else, and not away at all.

Regardless, I was unable to start right away with the first job due to a prior commitment that would delay my start date. I was steered towards something else. The prior commitment was that I needed to travel to Dallas. While in Texas, I felt very off balance. Alignment was interrupted with thoughts about this new, second job I was going to take. Every time I thought about the new job, I felt a sense of unease. I have learned that one of two things were happening. I was either thinking about the new job in the wrong way and needed to change my thought patterns, or I needed to make a physical change. While meditating on the two scenarios, I felt peace when I finally decided not to take the job, and I turned the position down.

I figured it was that particular job that I should stay away from, so I went on another interview. During the next interview, I felt very clear vibrations that I was not supposed to take that job either. After much alone time in alignment, I had an epiphany. I was not supposed to follow the same old protocol I had been following for most of my life. It became crystal clear to me that my time in Nevada should be centered around my emotional and spiritual growth; alignment; and my two children. So, I reluctantly stood still and allowed life to unfold around me.

The move has brought me closer to both of my children. This was indeed my initial objective, but as with any relocation, especially across the country, I have accrued some debt. Fortunately, this will be easily paid off over time. I am not only closer in proximity to my kids, but I have managed to strengthen my relationship with both of my children. I have learned two valuable lessons from relocating. First, I learned that being responsible with debt does not always mean it must be paid off immediately. Finances can sometimes wait. Time spent on my personal growth and time spent with my two children are paramount. The second lesson I learned is to trust in alignment. The false, egoic self that lives the same patterns over and over within me had to be terminated. This might sound a bit dramatic, but this became a priority. I knew the inner calling. I was sensitive to it now.

This led me to understand what is meant to fear the Lord. There is no need to go into an explanation for that other than, you reap what you sow. I did not want to sow another dysfunctional seed by my lonesome, egoic self. This time, Source Energy and I tag-teamed this co-creation and its harmony was felt in the vibrations deep within my soul. I felt the peace that passes all understanding.

It is only through alignment that you are able to discern these things. Without alignment, old, habitual patterns of fear lead the way. I am strangely confident in a way I have never felt before. I await the next challenge in my life, which will most certainly come. I look forward to it, not so much for the challenge, but more for the depth the challenge will take me. Being here on earth is not just for recreation, although that is certainly a secondary aspect. Our real purpose is to allow the universe to shine through us. This is accomplished simply by dropping the false self. Eventually, you will recognize the false self through alignment.

I have thought about my time on earth coming to an eventual end. I have asked myself, what would I do today if I knew I was going to die tomorrow. My answer is - to be aligned. Whatever comes from a life of alignment will be wonderful. Living from a place of peace is the most important objective. Any worldly activities that arise from my inner place of peace are welcome, but certainly are not necessary.

Chapter Fourteen

FLOWING ENERGY

The physical world responds directly to our core vibration, even if our core vibration is being subconsciously emitted. What is residing on the inside of you, comes out. The very thing a person is attempting to conceal from themselves or from the world, is emitted to the universe in the form of a vibration. A person's deepest, darkest secrets play a role in the vibration they emit, but the key to changing that vibration is not in the exposure of those secrets to the world. By secrets, I mean anything that is based in fear. Whatever you attempt to hide from yourself, and the world, will inhibit you from alignment. You will not need to tell anyone about your darkest fears or secrets to escape them. You only need to bring them into the mental space of alignment. In doing so, the awareness will extinguish them, and the chains of bondage will be broken.

The specific, physical, tangible, and worldly reason for the subconscious vibration of fear does not matter. Fear of failure, self-doubt, financial or sexual insecurities, etcetera, makes no difference. It is the *vibration* of fear that places limitations on an individual, not the specific fear itself. The vibration limits the person. When you have no idea what could possibly be limiting you, it is best to stop all thoughts for a short time each day to remove the negative energy that blocks the natural giving and loving energy flow.

Contrary to the worldly ways to gain or attain anything, when aligned, the universe "gives" without any effort on the part of the individual. The natural state of the universe is a giving and loving one. Humans have developed the idea of no pain, no gain. That is human "efforting" that can be pleasing and fun but is not necessary for a loving and fulfilled life. When this natural state of giving is found, you realize the things withheld from you in life that you struggled to receive, were the result of negative vibrations.

It does not take effort in the form of struggle and pain to make things happen. Actions do arise from effort but while aligned, this effort feels easy like the artist who has stayed up all night finishing the masterpiece. It takes the removal of the false self and the negative energy that comes with it. The universe's natural default mode is giving. Plants and birds receive necessary nourishment without struggle, begging, or pleading. We, too, have the ability to live freely. No anxiety, fear, struggle, lack, or effort is needed, necessary, or even felt, to obtain what the universe has predetermined to be solely yours. No other person can take from you what truly belongs to you. You have the power to block the flow of abundance to yourself or to allow your cup to overflow.

Abundance and love are freely flowing to everyone. It is like a never-ending waterfall. It continues to pour into life. We block that love from reaching us through misalignment to the world. When we align with Source, we allow abundance to begin to flow again. We do not need direction, clarity, or purpose, in advance of alignment to begin receiving our heart's desires. Those things are made clear to us while in alignment. It is through alignment that we receive all things including direction and purpose for our lives.

The moment one asks, the universe gives, but not always as quickly as a vending machine, although miracles do happen. For me, the universe responded only as quickly as I was willing to receive, which was slowly at first. I hesitated to release all the fear inside me. Much like a beginner swimmer might let go of the side of the pool for just a moment and quickly return to the safety of the poolside, I would try out "no fear/no thought" for just a moment. Eventually, I was able to release all fear that stopped the flow of abundance into my life. The default human condition is programmed to not be able to see the blessings right in front of our faces. Sometimes this is because we are too busy comparing ourselves to others. Either way, through alignment, all things are realized, including our own blessings.

Chapter Fifteen

THE RUNAWAY MIND

The first ten years of my life were absolute bliss. My neighborhood was new and there was always someone's house under construction. I spent countless hours playing in mile-high piles of dirt. As I got a little older, I went from playing with Matchbox cars to riding on real dirt bikes. I was truly dropped into my "earth suit" with the innocent mindset that comes with being a kid. Life was an extraordinary environment in which the word fear had no existence – however, this mindset did not last forever.

Somewhere around the age of ten, I lost my connection to this God energy that made me feel invincible. As I reached school age, fear took hold of me and I began to believe more in the egoic, false self than the God essence from which I came. In the blink of an eye, I left that peaceful energy source behind me and began drinking the world's Kool-Aid. At the time, I had no idea where I had gone wrong. Now, I know that in my mind, I traded in my God-given peace for a belief in the physical realm that proved so strong that I disassociated my true essence from my physical self.

I was denying my true self from a mental place of fear. This was not intentional or even recognized by me at the time. I identified with the physical form entirely and was scared. No other creation on earth can do this. A tree is unable to dislike itself or separate itself from the creator.

A tree simply is itself. Even animals do not do this unless they have lived closely enough to humans to adopt the mental position from the owners they live with. Animals will lose a limb or be placed in a new home without ever feeling sorry for themselves. They simply do not forget that they are the essence from which they were created.

It would take thirty-five more years of suffering through divorce, a devastating spinal injury, deep financial debt, the loss of a twenty-one-year career, the loss of my relationship with my children, and an alcohol addiction, before I would realize that my runaway mind had been the culprit. I recently joined a meditation group that correctly points out that I am at fault for everything in my life. I now agree wholeheartedly.

At the same time my physical world was crumbling, a dim, and barely detectable light of Consciousness, was creeping in. I did not know it back then, but it was definitely a helping hand reaching into my life. Very small things popped into my life that gave me some relief. Like the story of when I was a truck driver, driving home from Vermont. During that eight-hour ride, I listened to something other than my usual. The positive nature of the talk radio station not only captivated my mind, but it also indirectly stopped my mind's habitual form of negative self-talk. After eight hours of no news or self-talk garbage, I arrived at my destination feeling a sense of peace that I had not felt in a long time.

No circumstances had changed in my life, but I began to notice the correlation between eight hours of purposefully thinking about good things and the better moods I was having. This was my first introduction to the idea that one could feel good despite the circumstances. Over the next few years, I made myself my own guinea pig and tried new mind activities while muddling my way through a horribly, broken life. I wanted to feel like I was on vacation at all times, despite my circumstances.

At the tender age of ten, I created my false, egoic self based on a foundation of fear, anxiety, depression, and anger. I am fifty years-old now. What a wonderful journey it has been to discover that God lives within me. Thank God for the mess in my life that brought me back to the peace that the ten-year-old boy playing on the dirt pile knew so well.

I found a way to defeat depression, anxiety, fear, and anger. I am developing relationships based on my new vibrations of peace and love. Life is a wonderful place to be. No more struggle and strain. No more agonizing insomnia or overeating. I love myself and the world once again. I believe that some may find peace through much less tyrannical ways than I did, but for most, the road to dropping negative emotions will be a long one. That being said, I am enjoying the fruits of life now and the journey was well worth every second of deep, self-introspection and humbling moments of enlightenment.

Chapter Sixteen

JOE & GOD

Why would alignment be the answer to everything? Alignment is the practice of listening to the One Consciousness and aligning yourself to it through a vibration. The One Consciousness is not some sort of leader in the world, it is the world. It is the universe. It is all things.

Our limited mind cannot fathom infinity and therefore needs boundaries. The explanation of the One Consciousness I am about to give is not exactly correct because it cannot be defined. I provide this definition hopefully to help you understand.

Imagine the human body with all its cells, atoms, and electrons. Each one of the body's tiny atoms or cells could be a human. Let's call a small cell in the foot, Joe. Joe is doing his cellular job of going to work every day. Joe eats breakfast, delivers blood and oxygen for his career, comes home, and repeats the next day.

Joe's life seems routine until one day he flows through the bloodstream to the outside world through a small cut in the human's foot that he resides in. Remember, Joe is not the human, he is the cell inside the human. Joe represents you and me. We are a small piece of a larger, complex whole. In this example, the human with the cut foot that Joe (i.e., the cell) slipped through to the outside of the body, is the One Consciousness. Once Joe has an "out of body experience" he can see the big picture. Joe now knows the "truth." His life as a cell carrying blood and oxygen is not all there is.

Once outside the body, Joe is able to hear the voice of the One Consciousness. Remember that in this example, the human is God or the One Consciousness. There is a lot about this example that is wrong, but the point I am trying to make is that the One Consciousness encompasses everything, and you and I are infinitesimal in comparison, however, we are also an integral part.

It is best to just "be." We are human "be"- ings, after all. To exist without judgments, labels, and past or future thoughts is divine. You and I are part of an evolving universe. We have the freewill to think we are separate or connected to it. We have the freewill to align with the universe, or not. Our role on earth is not to compare and compete unless that ability does not exist for you yet. Humans have a strange way of feeling better about things. For example, someone suffering from a chronic condition may feel slightly better when the ailment has simply been given a name by a doctor.

Chronic, self-inflicted pain that many humans suffer is, in a way, our metamorphosis from the caterpillar to the butterfly. We may feel better knowing that the suffering, in the form of anxiety, depression, and anger, has a doctor-prescribed name. You are "becoming." In the earlier example, Joe (i.e., the blood cell), left the human body (i.e., the One Consciousness) through a small cut on the foot. Joe does not have a heart and lungs. He is a cell. Once he leaves the body (i.e., the One Consciousness) he will suffer from the lack of the life sustaining environment from which he came.

Joe's departure from the body is a step in his evolution. His existence outside the body may change to create the ability to adapt, overcome, and survive in this new dimension. This evolution is happening to you and me. Our suffering is part of our development. We are evolving to become more conscious humans. In the example, Joe is suffering without lungs but eventually, he will be made whole, healed, and will live in harmony with the One Consciousness.

The more we fight and resist the changes in our lives (i.e., our evolution) the more suffering we will endure. Insomnia, anxiety, depression, and anger will persist. Joe will suffer if he resists the adaptations, like the development of a heart and lungs. He will need his own heart and lungs to survive outside the body. Remember, Joe is the cell in the example. He has a choice to accept the changes to his cellular body, or not. He does not know that he will not survive outside the body without a heart and lungs, so he resists the metamorphosis. People do not grasp that we cannot just survive but we can thrive on earth through a type of mental metamorphosis of our own. Some do not realize peace is first obtained in the heart before being manifested in the world. A shift needs to be accepted or suffering will continue.

As long as you and I resist the metamorphosis, we will suffer. The suffering is there only for as long as we allow it to be there. We can escape our suffering by doing something we are not used to doing. As in the example, the only way Joe will stop suffering, is to do something he is not used to doing. He will have to use the newly created lungs to breathe. He may not want to use the lungs because while inside the body, his oxygen was given to him. He may die without ever utilizing this new way to live. Eventually, more cells like Joe will leave the body, and will learn to evolve after watching many resist evolution.

Take this moment to stop the resistance. Stop and look at nature or just use your five senses to steer the mind away from its old tendency to be on autopilot. You are like Joe. At this very moment, you can free yourself simply by allowing the changes. You can accept the change, or not. The choice is yours. Some may think that aligning to the One Consciousness means leading a dull and boring life while sitting cross legged in prayer 24/7. That is not true. Living a life while aligned can be as exhilarating or as laid back as you want. Your unique desires are given to you by the One Consciousness. Aligning with it, means you are able to experience life in exactly the way you want.

Living in alignment means that you get to experience life according to your uniqueness and you have the help of the universe to guide you. It means taking the fleshly, egoic and false leader off the throne. It means removing the limited and blind ego and allowing the one who created all, to direct your footsteps. Your ego is clever, but true fulfillment is found in the journey of life while in complete sync with the all-knowing one. When aligned, the One Consciousness will fulfill the desires of your heart in ways your limited and clever mind cannot fathom. Life is easier because you have the help of the one who knows it all. Trust in this entity is formed slowly as one gradually allows life to unfold as it should.

My daughter and I recently reconnected. I allowed the universe to handle life for the last six years. I wanted to scoop my two children up at the time of my divorce, but something told me to allow it to progress on its own. I allowed my children to choose and the choice they made was to live with their uncle in Las Vegas. My two children moved 2,500 miles away from me, but I trusted the One Consciousness for their safety. Back then, I did not know that was what I was doing. I just felt like it would be best not to introduce my personal feelings and desires into the mix of divorce. I somehow knew that if I forced them to share their time between their mother and I, it would cause more disharmony. I reluctantly, but peacefully let my children go.

After many years of working on harmonious thoughts and vibrations, I reconnected with my daughter. I was living on the Eastern Shore of Maryland at the time. I would walk the boardwalk and have long, incredibly deep conversations with Hannah. It was wonderful. She would tell me that she needed to speak with me because she felt calm around me. After a couple months of reconnecting with her and rebuilding my financial base, I bought a house in Las Vegas close to where both of my children were living. They lived with their uncle. Their mother was living on the east coast. I surprised them on a Saturday with the walk-through of the new, four-bedroom house. Once again, I had no intention of forcing them to live with me, but I bought a four-bedroom just in case they wanted to move in.

There were too many emotional triggers for Hannah to bear and consequently, she stopped speaking with me. I continued to build a relationship with my son, Nick. We rode mountain bikes together, jumped from a perfectly good airplane, and hit the gym. Two weeks before Hannah decided to move to Maine, she replied to me and agreed to take a trip to see the 2,200-year-old sequoia trees in California. It was a magical trip where we both felt the presence of God. While meditating 8,000 feet atop a mountain she said to me, "I can feel you. I can sense your presence." While on that trip, I promised myself I would allow every moment to be just as Universal Consciousness would want it to be.

That trip was a sign from the universe that following its methods, rather than my egoic ways, is best. I still felt a bit unsure about completely trusting in the process of Universal Consciousness. There was still a portion of me that could not completely let go. Hannah and I continue to build our relationship and it is wonderful. Nick and I spend time together as well. Our relationship is very rewarding. Aligning with the universe does not mean that we make right or wrong decisions. It allows the love of patience and the peace that passes all understanding to operate. In my case, allowing the universe gave room for healing after the destructive, egoic and false self attempted to create a life for me. The egoic plan obviously did nothing except inflate my ego, cause disharmony, and allow my fall from the egoic high in the form of divorce and so on.

When you are just starting to allow the universe into your consciousness through listening, the old, egoic ways will dissipate. It will take time to get your old, destructive vibrations to slow. It will take time for destructive manifestations to stop rising from the old vibrations of discord. It is hard to hand over control to the universe when more "so-called" bad stuff shows up in your life, but just know it is likely from the vibrations of the past self. I had forty or so years of egoic vibrations to work through before the harmonious vibrations could show up. Be patient with yourself. Small areas of trust will show themselves to you. Take those baby steps first.

Chapter Seventeen

MERGING WORLDS

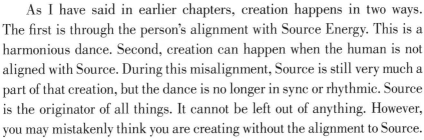

As I have said in earlier chapters, creation happens in two ways. The first is through the person's alignment with Source Energy. This is a harmonious dance. Second, creation can happen when the human is not aligned with Source. During this misalignment, Source is still very much a part of that creation, but the dance is no longer in sync or rhythmic. Source is the originator of all things. It cannot be left out of anything. However, you may mistakenly think you are creating without the alignment to Source.

Life becomes a practice of effort and struggle as creation is made without the alignment to Source, or so you may think. The disharmony is within the individual as you work and struggle to create. There is no disharmony in Source Energy. The world simply is as it should be. As you separate farther and farther from Source, an egoic illusion of freedom appears. You will continue with your life as the subtle whispers of Source begin to call you back into alignment. These whispers come in the form of negative energy that produce low levels of discomfort within the body. They are small signals informing us we have either lost our physical way or our thoughts are not in alignment with Source. As time goes on and we ignore these signals, the signals intensify and become larger disruptions in our lives. Ultimately, this creates suffering. In my case, I was so disconnected with the body's signals, it took my world imploding to create enough suffering to wake me up. All of which were my fault.

Some of the material things I lost have been restored to me. That feels good. Being aligned with Source has made me whole and complete without the need for completeness to occur in the physical realm of material things. Before I restored the relationship with both of my children, I wrote the next paragraph. I am leaving it in the original format because it shows the importance of not interfering with what is.

Restoring the relationship with my children would bring me great joy, but in it of itself, is not necessary for my inward happiness. If that were the case, I would continue to be a burden on them and the world. A sense of neediness, victimhood, low self-esteem, and disapproval of life would send vibrations to Source Energy from my lack of alignment with it. To those living from a place of the ego, those words may sound unempathetic and rash, that is okay. I am not trying to win you over or even win my children over. True love is being in alignment to Source through which all of creation flows. True love is unconditional. The deepest part of me, that is connected to Source, loves Source and all creations unconditionally. I do not need life to be a positive experience in order to feel peace, with the emphasis on the word "need." I would like for life to be positive and beautiful. I would like to have a great relationship with my children. I would like for the hungry people in the world to be fed. But, to feel dissatisfied with life in such a way that it causes disharmony within myself, is to align with the ego. I no longer "need" life to go my way in order to feel good. That would be conditional love. If that is what is inside of me, that is what I will create in the world. I will create conditional relationships and so on.

This is the perfect example of creating through the ego without alignment to Source. Source will gladly, unconditionally, love me enough to allow me to do what I please, even if it appears dysfunctional. On the other hand, Source will also love me enough to gently nudge me, in the form of negative emotions, back to alignment with it. Source loves us all too much to let us leave its infinitely loving arms without at least letting us know we are on the wrong track.

When we operate from a place of rest, within the alignment to Source, we create harmony inside our bodies and allow life to unfold around and through us. It is through this harmony that we feel complete, while Source is creating its masterpiece. Remember, Source is always creating through us. We can ignore that, create from a place of thinking that we are the *only* creator, feel the separation from Source in the form of low frequency negativity, and Source will still create through us.

In that way, life will not feel like a dance between your inner individual emanation of Consciousness and Consciousness itself. It will feel like a drag. Life will feel as if you are fighting it. Life will feel as if you are in prison. You might look out at the world and ask, "Why are you doing this to me?"

It is necessary to see how the inner and the outer realms are related in order to make changes in your life. The inner mental world, when aligned with Source, is the true world. The inner world when not aligned with Source is a false representation of the world. The outer world is a projection of one of these inner worlds. When you feel negative emotions, based on a thought that is not aligned with Source or an action not aligned with Source, it is a signal to get back to alignment.

After the practice of staying in alignment, even the slightest hint of negative emotion is all that is needed to realize you are either *thinking* something or *doing* something not in alignment with Source. Your sensitivity is turned up. The outer physical world of life becomes balanced on the inner alignment. Navigating our physical world is done through the emotions that come with inner alignment. The "need" for anything in the outer physical and material world drops away. The word need implies that we will be an internal mental mess without it. Besides the basic necessities, like food and water, most physical needs stem from an inner cavity or void. Searching the outside world for something is usually done to fill emptiness on the inside. Material things are wonderful additions to the person aligned with Source, but they are not necessary for fulfillment in the same way someone not aligned with Source needs the outer world for fulfillment.

The basis for determining which direction to take, according to your emotions, is part of the dance we do in life as a spiritual being navigating a physical world. Rather than getting our directions for life solely from our education and carefully thought-out calculations, we can incorporate the help of Universal Consciousness. This is done through alignment. It is obvious to most that the traditional method of combining prayer with a thoughtful and organized plan is a good way to go about making decisions.

In some cases, prayer is thought of as communication between two separate entities - the person and God. Alignment is the act of rejoining who you already are.

A better way to make decisions is by aligning with Source. Once aligned in a peaceful state of mind, notice your emotions as you think on one subject at a time. Whatever decision you are working on, think on that decision while in alignment. Remember, alignment is a relaxed state of mind where the connection between your consciousness and Universal Consciousness come together. This is the basis for love. You are not aligned if you deeply feel negative emotions as part of your identity when there is no thought. Negative emotions may arise while in that state of mind, but they will not stay in the mind. When aligned, they will be easily passed over as not being the true source from which you came.

Once truly aligned, ask yourself a question. It can be anything. "What will I wear tomorrow, or will I have enough money to pay the bills?" Universal Consciousness is pure love. You will be directed through love, not fear. If you are in true alignment and fear is sensed when bringing up your question, then one of two things is happening. The thought you are feeling is not in alignment with Source, or the subject matter is not in alignment with Source. Once again, become still and aligned and ask if the way you are approaching the subject is incorrect. Notice your emotions. Universal Consciousness always directs through love - never fear. When I felt a strong pull to move from the east coast of the United States to the west, it came with a peaceful presence. Even though it was a bit scary, while in alignment, I felt the peace that passes all understanding. Before alignment, I made quick, rash decisions based on fear. Decisions made from fear are acts of running away from something, not running towards something. Universal Consciousness will have us running towards something with a deep-rooted feeling that comes with peace. It is true that Source Energy will steer us away from harmful situations, but I have never been guided in any other direction except towards something peaceful. That is not to say you should not run from an unsafe situation. If you face the possibility of being physically harmed, running away is probably the only option.

The dance that happens when one is aligned, fulfilled, and content, while effortlessly "living your life" is wonderful. Life becomes effortless. Being in alignment does not mean being on a physical vacation where there are drinks to sip and waiters to serve you. It means having the vacation mindset while traversing life's ups and downs. It means living life from a place of trust, fulfillment, and contentment. An awareness of love and peace is felt. The push, pull, ups, and downs that used to come with life seem to cease to exist. There never was any reason to feel the anxiety I used to feel. It is through this alignment that the bliss of living is enjoyed. We become able to express those unique parts of ourselves and it is fulfilling to do so. Maybe a long time ago you were ridiculed for the way you thought about something or how you did something. Maybe you are self-conscious about the way you look or your career choice. When aligned, you realize that the things about you that are different from others are, in fact, the things that fulfill the intentions of Consciousness when you were created. If the rose was supposed to look like the sunflower, Consciousness would have made them the same. True bliss comes from knowing your uniqueness is a gift and, to express it from a place of peace, is fulfillment.

Furthermore, when life is lived through the unique expression of oneself, in conjunction with alignment, right and wrong fade away. I finally realized that nothing is more important than alignment. Not the need to be right, nor the need to express. If I feel negative emotions, I know I have either lost my physical and material way, or I have thought about something in a way that is contrary to Source Energy. Life's physical, material, and outward dance is steered by an internal process of staying aligned. The old way was in the pursuit of something fulfilling. The new way is to allow Consciousness to express itself through the unique form it has created (i.e., as the person) and enjoy being the witnessing presence during its fruition.

All human traits of negativity, anxiety, fear, greed, and guilt melt away as you realize the depth of who you truly are. A deep trust and completeness are found in this wisdom. For me, trust was the key to setting myself free. I spent most of my life in a state of fear and anxiety. Again, trust is the opposite of fear. It was through this knowledge that I realized the insanity of "no trust." Trust is all one can really do. Anything else is an illusion. Not to trust in the One Consciousness that made me, you, our thoughts, the planet, and so forth is the basis for anxiety. How can we not trust that life will be lived through us? Part of the human problem is wanting. We want things a certain way and we do not want other things. It is not until we understand our true essence that we finally agree with its desire to live life through us. We finally relinquish the illusion of control that we thought we had and allow Consciousness to just *be*.

Consciousness was always living life through us anyway. Consciousness expresses itself through us, even when we thought we were in control. Freedom comes with this knowledge and living a life with this in mind. Fear, struggle, and suffering become an illusion just as is the fictitious monster hiding under the child's bed. Just as foolishly as a child may think that the thin layer of cotton blankets they pull over their head will protect them from monsters, adults living from the false self foolishly think the false, egoic self is protecting them.

Chapter Eighteen

EVERYWHERE I GO, I AM

Have you noticed how easily you can become frightened while watching a horror movie? Your entire body composition changes. Your heart rate and breathing accelerates. The movie is not real, and you know this, but your body reacts like it is real. We can experience this same phenomenon when feeling negative emotions.

Chronic anxiety and depression act just like the scary movie except there is no movie to spark our body's reaction. Our thoughts create the body's reaction. Over time, a deeply rooted habit is formed, and your thoughts, mind, and body are creating depressive and anxious events all on its own. I am not referring to obvious, traumatic events happening in the current time frame, but if you are still reliving what happened to you years ago, you might be stuck in one of these chronic, habitual, and subconscious patterns.

Our lives are short. I am fifty years old, and I am just figuring out that many years of my life were spent feeling awful because my mind was addicted to anxiety. All on its own, my body was experiencing habitual patterns of negativity. Insomnia kept me from seeing clearly. Lack of sleep distorts our perception of the world. Drugs, alcohol, medications, and therapy did not cure me.

What do you do when your body and mind are creating overwhelming emotions of fear, anxiety, depression, insomnia, and anger? It feels very real because the emotions are real. Just like the effects of the horror movie, our emotions are real reactions to a fictitious experience. I used to have severe anxiety attacks out of nowhere. I tried hard to find out what was causing them. I tried hard to get rid of them. Nothing worked until I separated myself from *myself* through two minutes of mental training seven days a week.

Changing the negative patterns would require the exact formula that was used to create them. Negative emotions are created by making a habit out of them. We make the groove in the record deeper each time we repeat the negative song. The way to reverse this is also done through repetition, but now we need to focus on the positive until feeling good becomes the new habit. I found that I was placing more importance on figuring out why this was happening to me rather than changing anything. Again, it is better to stop the bleeding before chasing the shooter. This is also true for negative emotions, but I was so desperately caught up in feeling bad and wanting answers, I did not have the energy or desire to do the mental work.

I did not love myself enough to want to do the mental work. I was drowning in despair and insomnia, and I was searching for a quick fix. I just wanted someone to give me a pill or hand me a miracle. We need to love ourselves enough to do the mental work. It is hard and takes courage, but time is running out. We all have been diagnosed with a life-threatening disease - it is called life. This life will end eventually and when it does, I do not want to say that I waited for happiness, but it never came. Millions are suffering with anxiety, depression, insomnia, and so on. Take two minutes every day to work on yourself. You are worth it. Your life is worth it. The more people that practice alignment, the more others will see that true freedom exists. You will be helping the world to become a better place through your own alignment. Let your light shine.

The universe has an enormous amount of love, peace, security, protection, and guidance for each and every one of us. The universe gives you the freewill to choose peace even while the horror film is playing on the screen. Do you love yourself enough to take two minutes and retrain your brain every day? I know you are tired, but it is the only way I know how to break free from the struggle with the fictional film of fear.

The mental aspect of this is the hard part. There is nothing that is physically taxing. As a matter of fact, the hardest part is doing the mental work and allowing life to unfold through you. The old me hated this. I was so used to struggling and striving. The new me recognizes that I am still working hard but find myself embraced by the loving arms of Source Energy. In this way, it does not feel like hard work because my old self categorized "hard work" as suffering and paying my dues. When we work hard through alignment with Source, it feels easy and almost effortless. The old, hardworking me thought I had to experience pain to have gain. I repeated this erroneous thought over and over to myself.

Inside each and every one of us is a beautiful life of abundance and peace and it comes quite effortlessly through alignment. The false self may tell you that this is not possible, but it is only through alignment that you will know which path is correct. All answers come through alignment to Source. You will know when to take physical action and when to rest. Guidance will come from a place of peace, never fear. Actions taken through alignment that appear to be a mistake are, in fact, a part of the fruitful journey. It is only through alignment that one knows this to be true. When aligned, you connect your individual and unique expression of the One Consciousness to Universal Consciousness. When doing so, you lose your identity, embrace truth, and you are able to feel your way through life. The human body is an instrument used for guidance.

Remember, Source is always acting through us. We may not know that we have Source Energy inside us because we are too busy living through the false self. We can choose to act without listening to the whispers of Source Energy. We have that right. After alignment to Source in my own life, I noticed the difference between the old actions taken without alignment and the actions inspired through alignment. Actions taken without alignment feel like struggle. My old, egoic self-loved struggle, especially when I would defeat or conquer something. This type of action places unnecessary stress on the body which can eventually lead to physical ailments.

While operating from my false self, I noticed a string of "bad luck" that I attached to events or actions. My body was deteriorating. My digestive track did not work well, and gastric issues ensued. Prior to alignment, I slept very little. My normal was to fall asleep for two or three hours only to wake up with a racing mind. After alignment, I sleep a solid night. I awake feeling healthy and whole. It seemed like life was never cooperative before alignment. After alignment, it feels like I have the best luck ever. Of course, there is no luck involved. I am aligned and listening to the direction of Source Energy. In this way synchronicities show up, not luck.

Through alignment my body has repaired itself. The lifelong run of bad luck has been replaced with good. My body works better while aligned. I began to use my body as a way to guide my mental self. The old way was to let the egoic mind tell my body what to do. My direction for life was based on inherited fears and guidance of those before me. They called it love. They would say, "I love you, that is why I am telling you this." As children, we follow the well-meaning advice of our influential leaders, parents, schools, government, and religion. The new way to live life through alignment is to follow the unique expression of yourself first, and then incorporate the well-meaning advice from the outside world, but only if it harmoniously resonates with you.

When traversing life through alignment, the body works and feels well, overall. I still have arthritis pain in my lower back on occasion, but it is not nearly as debilitating as it once was. Challenges still come to me, but I am safely in the loving arms and guidance of Source Energy. There is a deep feeling of peace that comes with alignment. It is as if I cannot get it wrong. It is as if I will always be on par for my life. Give it a try. Just two minutes a day will expose you to a whole new way to live. Take the time to love yourself enough to stop listening to the egoic, false self. Place importance on your essence and treat your physical body with love. Magical things happen when we align ourselves to the creator of the universe.

Healing, wholeness, love, peace, security, good health, good relationships, and gratitude will fill your mind. Life will unfold in a purposeful way, and the peace that passes all understanding will take over you in all circumstances. This is where I live now. I once heard someone say, "Everywhere I go, there I am." I used to take my false and egoic self to a new house, new car, new relationship, or new job. Everywhere I went, I still experienced incompleteness. Everywhere I went, there I was. I made the change to alignment. Now everywhere I go, I take the peace that passes all understanding with me. If I go anywhere in life, whether it be to a new relationship, job, or home, I now go for a different reason. The old self searched to find completeness, and even ran from the incompleteness. The new self is simply and effortlessly transitioning through life, already at peace and fulfilled. Now, everywhere I go, there I am. Now, this is a much better place to be, no matter where I am in the world physically.

Chapter Nineteen

RUNNING AWAY, STANDING STILL, OR RUNNING TOWARDS

The mind, when left to its own accord, has a built-in agenda. Without alignment to Source Energy, the mind operates out of sin. Sin is a word that comes loaded with a negative connotation. It is often a misunderstood word. When operating from the egoic mind, that is to say without alignment to Source Energy, one's identity is in the physical realm. To solely identify with the physical realm is to miss the mark. This is considered sinful. Unfortunately, people have misunderstood this and have associated guilt with sin. When the word sin is used, most get a sense of guilt and think of evil. Sin was never intended to be thought of in that way. Unfortunately, people feel it necessary to feel guilt for having taken part in doing something wrong, as if the guilt itself is the payment for the sin. Nothing will hold a person back more than the belief that guilt is a form of payment or that it is necessary in order to learn from a mistake. Guilt, in any way, shape, or form, is a negative emotion that removes the chance to learn from a mistake and move on. It is just another form of suffering created by the ego. If guilt is an immobilizing entity, it is not serving you well. Remember that negative emotions are just pointers. They are just here to remind us of when we have "lost our way." It is okay to notice the guilt within, learn your lesson, and release it or let it pass through you. If you still feel guilty about something that happened in the past, you could be keeping a diseased energy in your body.

The first hurdle to overcome is the misinterpretation of the word. Just know that to sin means to be unaligned with Source. In no way should one feel guilty, shame, or think of evil in the same sense as murder and other egregious acts. Preconceived ideas and conditioning from our past are an ignorance that will stand in our way of freedom if we do not learn to quiet our mind. It is in this stillness that we can uncover things that do not serve us well.

The mind has a habitual agenda that is completely comprised of the false self. The false self is not a bad thing, in terms of right and wrong. The term false self is not bad at all. It is just a way of saying that we have missed the mark. The egoic mind lives in the ignorance of the false self. When living our lives from this vantage point we see the world completely differently from the perspective of Source Energy. From the vantage point of the false self, we live in the dichotomy of opposites where there is right, wrong, comparisons, judgments, and labels.

It is inside the mindset of the sinner, the false self, or the ego (whichever term suits you) that the person is in a constant state of lack, running away, or needing more. There is a continual, underlying feeling of unease. The person is a slave to the ego. The person is at the will of the lost and false self that relives fears from the past and even the same achievements over and over from a deficient subconscious conditioning in the past - all the while trying to predict and shape the future as a means of protection. You will always be operating from a place of fear because you do not know your creator.

It is terribly difficult to get around the built-in agenda of the egoic self with the very same mindset that it operates on. It is like trying to get the correct answer to a math question by using a broken calculator. That is why it is imperative to quiet the mind. It is through the quiet mind that the veil of ignorance is lifted. One way to know if you are operating under the influence of Source Energy or the ego, is by checking in with your emotions, low-level feelings, and habits. Are you sensing a low-level state of lack and fear?

Some people may think that to be still means to do nothing. For our purposes, being still means to quiet the mind to a mental place of peace. Through the alignment with Source comes the creative, unconditioned thoughts that lead to doing something in the physical world. While we are actively doing whatever it is we were inspired by Source to do, we do it from a mental place of rest, peace, or stillness. When aligned, there is no stress while performing tasks. There can, however, be hard work, but sweat from the brow of a person creating while under the influence of Source, is not felt from stress and struggle. One can work hard when in the creative mode. Many wonderful paintings may have been created while aligned. Those creative masterpieces may have stolen some physical energy and perhaps the artist even lost some sleep during their completion, but to the creator, the effort was done in inspiration not desperation.

Creating or actively living from a place of rest may feel wrong to some. It certainly felt wrong to me. The first half of my life was spent doing things from a place of struggle. Again, my inner motto was one that resembled the phrase, no pain, no gain. Somehow, I got it in my head that I, myself, and my efforts were not good enough unless I lived up to some subconscious and nebulous belief about myself. You will know if you are living your life in alignment by the way the body is feeling and doing. When I am in alignment, my body works best. I sleep all night, desire healthy food, I am inspired to exercise, the digestive tract works well, the old pains of osteoarthritis diminish, and I generally feel appreciative and well. That is not to say physical challenges will not come. I have an injury above my knee that stopped me from riding my bicycle and a shoulder injury that required me to change my routine at the gym. The physical world is still presenting me with challenges. The difference is my inner self is okay with it.

In this way, we have a tool for guidance. The body will help steer us but remember that you are a unique and individual expression of the One Consciousness. It is imperative that you follow along with your uniqueness. If you try to be or do something because of others, you may get off track. In the same way the rose needs to express itself differently from the sunflower, you will need to follow that inner calling as well. This will, more than likely, be different from those around you. Negative emotions can be a friendly signal to wake us up to this fact.

There is no need for me to lose harmony with Source Energy just because I cannot ride my bicycle anymore. Alignment with Source feels better. Obviously, feeling bad about physically or mentally hurting another individual is not what I am talking about - it is only when we feel negative emotions based on old conditioning. I used to believe that unless I was struggling, I was not working or being productive. A conditioned, negative emotion would appear when I was not acting according to an old paradigm. This feeling let me know that I was not acting in accordance with alignment. No one but yourself will know whether or not you are in alignment.

The human trap is to look to the outer physical and material world for answers first. This could not be further from the truth. We must first look within and allow alignment to steer our physical footsteps in the material world. We could have a lot of options in the material world that all point to one path. Ignoring our inner wisdom, could quite possibly put us on the wrong path. Science told us that our heart and lungs did not have the capacity to allow a person to run a mile in under four minutes and yet it was accomplished by many. If all you do is search the internet, run your calculations, and follow what has already been established without consulting your higher self, you will miss the mark.

Balance with the practical world comes from inner stillness and alignment with your creator. The idea is to operate your entire life from a place of peace. This is completely contrary to what I learned early on, but once practiced, it feels familiar, like arriving home. It becomes as intuitive as riding a bike. Operating from a place of stillness is sanity, anything else feels like insanity. Love of self is seen differently. My old self used to say things like, "I will eat this huge meal because I worked hard, or I will stay up late watching movies because I deserve it." The aligned self gets great joy out of true love of self which is to say, "I will go to bed early because it is good for me, and I will feel better the next day."

It is amazing how much of a shift happens when one is aligned. It becomes more important to stay on the high vibration of love than to be right, get your point across, or anything else. With alignment comes knowing that out of love blooms more love. In the egoic state of mind, one might think it is necessary to struggle but that only creates more of the same - struggle. When we live by our higher calling, we live according to the laws of nature. Think about a tree or a stream - each lives effortlessly in abundance of only what is needed for its individual existence. If you make it a point to live from a place of stillness and thus, alignment, you will receive a heart full of appreciation. That is all that is needed for fulfillment on earth. Everything else is the icing on the cake. Life is already wonderful and adding anything more is just a bonus. Suddenly, time will be on your side. Synchronicity will accommodate you.

This did not come automatically for me and keeping the old, conditioned thoughts of struggle at bay is an ongoing process that needs a gentle reminder on occasion. It is no longer a battle, but it was at first. Now, it is effortless to live from a place of contentment and peace. Despite challenging moments that inevitably will arise, I know the answers are found within the mind of alignment.

It is in the stillness that all things are formed, answered, and uncovered. It is in the stillness that we will find a profound truth. Peace is already abundant within you. More importantly, you will discover that you are exactly where you are supposed to be. Consciousness cannot come to know itself through you unless you are aligned. You must be mentally still for this to happen. To put it another way, you have to go to Source Energy on Source's vibration. Begging God for help may not free you as fast as meeting God with a still mind, Source, or Consciousness on the vibration where Consciousness resides.

The fallacy is to think this god-entity thinks like we do. Placing Source in the limited box of our thinking will keep you stuck. We must go to Source on and in that mental, quieted mind in order to find peace and understanding. Begging God to intervene and physically change our life is a lengthier process for achieving peace. For me, that was the way I first discovered peace, but it led me through enormous amounts of suffering first. Now that I have experienced the peace that passes all understanding and suffering, I know what it takes to find the peace we are all searching for - it requires effort on our part.

Struggling with insomnia, suicidal depression, and severe bouts of anxiety, I searched for Source Energy with all my heart, soul, and mind. Eventually, I found what I was looking for, but it was not where I expected to find it. I was forced or compelled to look there - and that place was inside *me*. The other way to find peace is to stop the habitual thoughts all on our own. It requires you to do something that inside the clever, but limited mind, seems contrary to helping an individual and this is the biggest hurdle. Recognizing that we are getting in our own way, is key to making this mental shift.

Allowing your mind to run frenetically in worry leads to more physical movement in the world. Like running in place, the world will be less satisfying if you are uncomfortable inside your own mind. You may search the physical world for the latest and greatest. You might even search for new experiences and material things. You might think you are running towards these new things, when in fact, you may actually be running *away* from the mind. You may not be comfortable in the way your mind is processing the world around you. Anxiety, stress, over-eating, and so forth may result.

There is a big spiritual movement that has taken advantage of the ever-searching mind. As people become more and more uncomfortable with the way their mind processes their world around them, they step onto a "seeking treadmill" to nowhere with the hope that they will find what they are looking for in the outer world. Peace has to be obtained inside the mind for peace to show up in the physical world. As I have said earlier, not this book nor any other modality will give you exactly what you are looking for. All approaches can only *point the way*. Nearly everything in the physical and tangible world is a trap in that its promises are empty, including the words on these pages.

The way to fill the empty space in yourself is to realize the mind does not know what it is looking for. The mind and thoughts are just as much tangible physical matter as the world is. This is why the unbridled mind seeks fulfillment in the world. It is not the mind that is empty of fulfillment, it is the individual's alignment, but because our perception is mind-based, we wrongly seek on the mind's own level. Once we identify and fulfill the real place of emptiness, which is to know Consciousness once again, we complete ourselves. Once we are complete, there is no "neediness" in ourselves anymore. At this point, whatever the physical world offers, is appreciated, but is not necessary.

Chapter Twenty

PEACE VS. WORLDLY TREASURES

So, what does a person really "get" or receive by being aligned? What tangible, credible thing happens when a person devotes their life to alignment to Source Energy?

A person receives a gift far greater than they could ever imagine. The gift of peace and love. Peace and love are actually what many are searching for in the physical world when they dream of a spouse, new house, kids, and a great career. They just do not know it. They think fulfillment comes from those things. It is important to understand this aspect because this next point is a bit difficult to comprehend.

It is fun to live in this world through our ego until a major failure or fall happens. Living "egoically" means that a person feels very attached to the world and creations. Every loss or win is felt deeply, so deeply, you actually become the loss or the win. Some succumb to suicide as a result of loss. Others may turn to alcohol or work to cover up the pain of loss. Their identity is wrapped up in the loss or the wins and winning makes them feel superior.

While all of that may sound completely normal to most, none of that, including the wins, are the gift of peace and love that comes with alignment. Many may think of Heaven as a place where you will have everything your heart desires. The peace and love that comes with alignment is much greater than that. It is greater than any euphoric high you could imagine.

This major difference between the peace that passes all understanding, and the "wins" of the world are what makes some people overlook the precious gift that resides inside everyone's heart. We have all had moments in our lives where time seemed to stand still. We have realized a moment in time where clarity of our senses is felt or times when we felt free, for however brief of a moment. Maybe you had this feeling when you were married. Or perhaps you felt this during a near death experience like a car crash, or when jumping from an airplane.

These moments of clarity are the closest way I know how to describe the peace that passes all understanding. When examined closely these experiences really do not feel the same as purchasing a car or getting married. During that brief moment in time when you felt like the world stood still, you experienced a peace greater than any worldly euphoric high that might come with retail therapy. This is important because this feeling is similar to the one you will sense when you take just two minutes a day to stop the thoughts of judgments, labels, complaints, and drama.

There will be one part of you (i.e., the false self or the ego) that will not want to participate in a two-minute time out. That particular part of you is the part of you that you always listen to. It promises to keep you safe. It is also the reason you are still suffering with anxiety, depression, and insomnia. The other part of you wants a break. This part of you wants to sleep well, be at peace, and love life with the zeal of a small child.

You will know when you have found it. It will feel really good, but not like the euphoric high that comes with a new purchase. It could feel euphoric, but it will not be anything like you have ever felt before. The ego may talk you out of it once you find it. That was the case with me. I was walking through a park in northeast Las Vegas when I found what I always wanted. Although I did not know what it was at the time. I did not know that I would even want this feeling or that it even existed, but there it was.

The sky was crystal clear that day. The birds were singing loudly, and I heard them clearly. The smell of the trees and grass was nutty and pleasant. I left my body in a spiritual way. Not physically, but I was not the same Rob as before. I did not have a mental picture of the past that would hold me back, or of a future that would jeopardize my safety and cause me worry.

I was simply present, in peace and love. It did not last more than about three or four minutes because my ego jumped into my head and began to remind me that I had plenty to worry about.

It was a good lesson for me. I now know that I need to choose peace at every moment. This is not a one-and-done, fix-it-forever kind of fix. The peace you are searching for exists inside you. You will need to search for it with all your heart, mind, and soul. Not in a literal way, of course. The peace that passes all understanding cannot be found by analyzing and thinking. You kind of have to feel your way there. Once you have found it, you will know it. You will not question it. It is then up to you to take yourself there every second you can, throughout each and every day. Buddha said, "Peace comes from within, do not seek it without." These words now resonate more than ever.

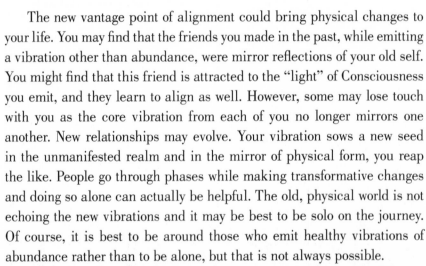

Chapter Twenty-One
WHAT'S NEXT?

The new vantage point of alignment could bring physical changes to your life. You may find that the friends you made in the past, while emitting a vibration other than abundance, were mirror reflections of your old self. You might find that this friend is attracted to the "light" of Consciousness you emit, and they learn to align as well. However, some may lose touch with you as the core vibration from each of you no longer mirrors one another. New relationships may evolve. Your vibration sows a new seed in the unmanifested realm and in the mirror of physical form, you reap the like. People go through phases while making transformative changes and doing so alone can actually be helpful. The old, physical world is not echoing the new vibrations and it may be best to be solo on the journey. Of course, it is best to be around those who emit healthy vibrations of abundance rather than to be alone, but that is not always possible.

Evolution will occur inside the mind and to the physical world. For me, not many friendships were formed while I was learning how to fly with my new wings. The caterpillar is alone during the metamorphosis into the butterfly. I was also in a solo phase of growth. Rest assured that when your head stops spinning from the many changes you go through, your core vibration will attract a new set of relationships and surroundings. Conversely, many things can and will stay the same.

The things that do change will mentally and/or physically further evolution through you. To the egoic mind, this may sound scary. To the aligned individual, it makes no difference. Alignment to the One Consciousness is the source of living water. The thirst for living water or anything else does not exist when aligned. To the aligned person, you are already abundant. It is through alignment that you will receive the peace that passes all understanding. Mentally and/or physically furthering evolution through oneself is not scary at all to the aligned person.

Once the thoughts are stopped, life will begin to change. Most likely, life will begin to change in unnoticeable ways. With me, the universe was responding to a mindset of fear and lack before I learned how to stop thought. The universe moves slowly. Like the growth of grass, you cannot see it if you are staring at it. If you come back a week later, you will see that it needs to be cut. Behind every thought is a universal movement of energy. If the thoughts have been negative for quite some time, the universe will have a momentum that is in direct response to the thoughts. This impetus will take time to slow.

Vibrations will change immediately according to your thoughts, but because of the past negative momentum, life may continue to unfold some negative manifestations that were previously deemed yours. Positive thoughts will obviously produce the like in physical manifestations. I did not have any idea what I wanted out of life. I was trying to change the negativity, and I had no idea how to be positive. It is completely okay to keep a still mind of no thoughts without placing positive energy into the practice of alignment.

Source Energy is love, and without giving it any positive direction in alignment, it will automatically slow, stop, and reverse that train full of negative gifts that was destined to be yours. It is perfectly okay not to know exactly what you want when aligned. Being aligned is harmonizing your consciousness with the One Consciousness. In this way, good and positive energy is being created and your "work" is complete. You can rest in the alignment, receive wisdom, and take whatever physical action is needed. As the more positive physical manifestations show up from the direct result of no thought, this reinforces the righteousness of the path.

Again, it is perfectly okay to stop thought without having a specific direction for your life. Source Energy will know what to bring to you. This developed the necessary trust I was lacking in my life. I simply stopped thought, gradually noticed the negative waves of manifestations slow, and was provided healthy physical manifestations in return. I began to notice that I was being taken care of. This took place over a time frame of six years. I stopped negative thinking many years ago merely by accident when driving that long trip home from Vermont.

I realized that it did not really matter how I stopped the thoughts, as long as it was with the high vibrations that come with alignment. Alcohol, drugs, and things of this nature, stir up low vibrations that stop thoughts and encourage no spiritual growth. Stay away from stopping thoughts with low vibrational methods. Staring at something and sort of "spacing out" is not the type of no thought I am referring to. This mental energy is pulsing and full of life when aligned. My entire well-being was better. I continued to redirect my thoughts in this way for several years. Things got slightly worse before they got better, but I believe this was due to the momentum of the already established negative energy. Eventually, my spine would become healed without the need for surgery. I quit drinking alcohol and I began to restore the relationships with both of my children.

The energy shifted on the inside before it made its way to my physical form. Getting started was not easy. I was so mentally and physically exhausted that I did not think there was any way I would be able to change my life. Turns out, the energy shift was physically easy. What was challenging was convincing myself that my situation would continue to change for the better just by saying affirmations and redirecting my thoughts. This appeared absurd to me. Persuading myself that this would work was harder than actually doing the mental exercise.

My trust in the universe was beginning to form. Although I knew anxiety was an illusion that I created, I would still have severe panic attacks on occasion. I believe this was due to the mind's habitual, addictive tendency to feed on those brain chemicals that were produced from the rising of the fight-or-flight patterns. I began to sit through these bouts of anxiety much like sitting through the delirium tremens, cold sweats, vomiting, and headaches that came with quitting alcohol. I knew this would eventually end. There were many late nights without sleep as I would wait out the mind's desperate calls to engage me in fits of anxiety at 2 am. I would simply refuse to lose my connection to Source Energy. At this point, I knew that keeping a healthy vibration was love of self. This was something I had never done before. That is, love myself enough to say no to any vibration other than love.

Many of us overeat, drink too much, or exercise too much. These are self-destructive acts of violence. On occasion, I would eat in the middle of the night when I could not sleep. These are all physical manifestations that form from not loving ourselves. True love is to love yourself so much that the love of self is unconditional to the manifestations of the world. This is very important and took me a long time to comprehend.

Most people feel it is completely justifiable to get upset if your car breaks down, you are late for work, or if the bills stack up. Getting upset elevates our blood pressure, can lead to nervous breakdowns, and even heart attacks. Did you know that when you live in alignment with Source Energy, you realize the challenges of the world are not meant to harm you, but instead strengthen your faith in the pure essence from which you evolve? Did you know that it is actually possible not to get upset over these things? Obviously, the loss of a loved one will produce great emotional pain, but that is not the challenge I am speaking of. It is noteworthy to say that when a loved one dies, our human hearts will deeply miss them, but our alignment with the One Consciousness from which they came, comforts us as its loving arms embrace our lost loved one in its eternal loving light.

It is not about staying positive. Do not get that confused with alignment. The feeling that comes with alignment has no opposite emotion in the way that a positive feeling does. Being aligned means allowing all things as they are, but more than that, it means allowing your own emotions to be as they are without being attached to them. I was upset for a brief moment when my truck's catalytic converter was stolen, in broad daylight, as I was participating in a Zoom meeting. The emotion that arose in me was noticed for what it was. I allowed it to be there much like I allowed the anxiety to rise up in me while I watched from a distance. Several minutes passed, and I drove the enormously loud truck to be repaired. While doing so, I revved the loud engine and shouted, "Yeah! Get some!" I knew that my core vibration was worth more to me than that catalytic converter. I loved myself enough to stay aligned.

Life becomes enjoyable again. A small child can be just as happy playing with a cardboard box as playing with an expensive toy. The joy of being alive is already in the child and it makes no difference what is happening around them, for the most part. I will say it again because it is very important. The abundantly joyful child playing with a cardboard box is joyful because they brought the joy with them. The joy was already *inside* them. If it was not, they would not be happy with the box. It is just a box. As adults, we can also experience this bliss. The reason we struggle to feel at peace is because we bought into the idea that material possessions mean more than internal peace. We truly forgot our own spiritual roots and see ourselves from a human perspective of comparisons, labels, and complaints. We identify with things of this world so strongly that if we do not have a certain something, we subconsciously think we are lacking, and this hurts our ego.

Some are surprised when they see a person who has nearly nothing, as happy, thinking, how could that be? Conversely, you might be surprised to see a wealthy individual, who is sad. This perspective is seen through the eyes of the ego. Looking at the world through the eyes of alignment creates a different view of the world. It makes total sense to see a wealthy person unhappy or a poor person filled with joy. Everything makes sense to the person who is aligned. Everything is an expression of the One Consciousness. That is not to say the person who is aligned is happy about everything. They are not. They are, however, at peace with everything. Much like the child who plays joyfully with the cardboard box, the person in alignment to Source Energy has the joy of peace in them already.

Look around. There are many outwardly healthy individuals who take medications to feel better. It is okay and justifiable to take medication for depression, anxiety, or any other issue. That is not the point I am trying to make. The fact is that some perfectly healthy individuals have created havoc in their own lives simply from the thoughts they think. I used to be one of them. These people are still looking to the physical world for answers. If a poor person can be completely at peace in life and a wealthy person commits suicide, and we are still dumbfounded as to how this could be, we have really missed the point. No physical thing can bring joy or take it away. Peace is inside the heart and comes with alignment to Source. It does not come with alignment to worldly things. Peace does not come when you know you have enough money or when you finally achieve something that appears to bring you security or love.

There are a ton of people agreeing with me right now and yet they are still operating in life much like a functioning alcoholic lives in denial. They nod their heads in agreement with their hands covering their eyes and say as the foolish child exclaims, "If I cannot see you, you cannot see me." I was one of those people too. I felt miserable on the inside but put on a façade. I truly thought that if I covered up my confusing pain, I would eventually find freedom. Hiding from our own delusion creates a roadblock. The only way around the mental roadblock of anxiety, depression, and other negative emotions is to go through the pain with your eyes wide open.

There is no magic pill for peace. You have to come boldly to the throne of Universal Consciousness, ask, and then receive. This is the part that eludes people, and me at one time. I questioned. As a matter of fact, I did a lot of questioning. I even begged for mercy. I begged for the suffering to end. The part I missed was the receiving part. It was not handed to me. Receiving peace is more like going to the hands of Source Energy and taking the item that has your name on it. Receiving is an act of faith that you need to do for yourself. As the saying goes, "You can lead a horse to water, but you cannot make it drink." The drinking part is much like the receiving part. The horse has to take the final step of drinking to receive the water. We have to receive the gift of peace by actually doing the receiving part.

People struggling with negative energy have no idea that they have been taken over by a subconscious force that will not let them see that they themselves are the reason for the suffering, and that they have the key to unlock the door to peace. I used to be one of them. I swore up and down that the world was doing this or that to me. I saw the world as a bad place. I hated when people would tell me that I was fabricating anxiety for myself. I would not listen to them. I would simply find another individual under the same negative energy source that I was, and we would share our beliefs in the hurtful world. The more a person filled with negative energy kicks and screams for help, the more negative energy is dumped onto the individual. Why? Because their inner vibration of fear is sent out to the universe and the universe responds with the like.

No one can help the person suffering on the physical plane because that person is like a power station creating his/her own negative energy stream. An aligned person can shine a light on this suffering individual, and one of two things will happen. The suffering person will either see the light or leave. The light is healing but if you are suffering and are not ready to be healed, that is, if you are not finished suffering, you will not accept peace.

Life after stopping thought and alignment, is receiving. For some, this concept is terribly difficult to grasp because of innate feelings of unworthiness. Worthiness is of the heart, and not of material things. Your notion of your own personal worth begins in your mind. Mistakenly, some wait for others to dictate their worth. While aligned with Source, you will receive your worthiness. It is of a divine nature. Try not to think about worthiness in the way we often do, from a worldly perspective. For example, when you take a test, your performance will dictate worthiness and a corresponding grade will be assigned, but that is not it at all. Receiving the peace that passes all understanding through worthiness is accomplished just like a baby innately knows he/she is worthy of God's love. Imagine looking into a baby's eyes. What do you see? Love, of course. You do not even question it. That baby knows love and worthiness without ever needing to pass a test or to prove anything. We can attain the peace that passes all understanding through alignment, acknowledging our worth, and receiving. You do not need to do or prove anything at all. You already are enough, exactly the way you are. Material objects are not necessary to accept peace. You are pure love. It is not only okay to drop the illusion of having to prove, strive, struggle, and attain, it is necessary. Comparisons, labels, complaints, achievements, future goals, finances, and memories of dysfunction have ZERO impact on receiving the peace that passes all understanding right now.

Rather than people filling their mental head space with love, which includes forgiveness, they attempt to patch up the mental wound with a physical object, all the while denying the emptiness inside and living from their false self. Alignment is the only way. The physical modality one uses to become aligned is of no consequence. Life after quieting the mind is all about alignment on the inside. It is all about keeping the love vibration going. Retaining pain and suffering is not unconditional love of self. Do not get hung up on words and methodologies. You must find within you that place of peace through whichever method resonates best. This book may spark something within you. You may discover parts of the book that do not work with you. Do not get caught up on the stuff that does not harmonize with you. Doing so will keep you stuck. Allow this book to ignite that spark within you. Forget about the things that do not resonate and move forward on your own journey.

You have decided to love yourself *conditionally* when you stop alignment. Your love of self is conditional on your circumstances and, in most cases, conditional on your own thoughts. Many are not purposefully denying themselves love in this way. Many have built their lives on deep, subconscious negative beliefs and are completely unaware of it. Once all thoughts cease, alignment can be realized, and healthy vibrations can be emitted from your heart. It is only then will you realize just how deeply ignorant you have been. It was certainly shocking to me.

I did not realize why I was still receiving the world's negative energy until I stopped thought. It was then that I noticed that I was sending vibrations of desired love on top of the subconscious vibrations of fear that started when I was younger. The mask of my own false self was hidden from me. It is nearly impossible to see one's own mask. With alignment comes freedom to truly trust in the One Consciousness and know that your own consciousness is being loved, guided, and helped. There is no end to the practice of alignment and stopping thoughts. This practice continues, but not from a place of suffering and lack as it once did.

Life is no longer a means to an end. Time is no longer against us. Source has extended its loving arms. In Source's hand is an abundance of everything you have asked for, plus even greater things. It is up to you to take from the hand and receive. For me, I felt like time was restricting me in some way. I used to feel like I had to rush through things - as if time were against me. As I spent more time in alignment, I discovered that I was rushing myself in all areas, including small areas. I would even rush while brushing my teeth. This mindset was a conditioning from the past. I was in fear that I would lose out somehow and that the only way to stay ahead was by hurrying up.

As time went on, I would need to periodically remind myself to observe my own behavior for a sense of rushing. Most of the time I was rushing for no reason. Eventually, I did not need to monitor my behavior anymore. It became natural for me to be at peace nearly all of the time. For me, the most important thing was to second guess all of my behaviors at first. I learned that my mind could not be trusted. I found that my mind, when left to its own devices, as I did for the first half of my life, would create stress, all the while claiming that it was protecting me. I also learned to forgive myself for this behavior. I realized just how much of a burden I was to myself and others. I learned that I was the reason for all of the experiences in my life - good *or* bad.

As life continued on after this initial awareness, I learned things about myself on a gradual basis. I learned that I valued others' opinion of me before my own wellbeing. I actually valued darn near everything more than myself. I used to devote the majority of my energy to the false self and to what I thought was the opinion of others. Steeped in low self-esteem and self-destructive behaviors that were hidden from me, was a sort of subpar baseline vibration for living. Undetectable to me, was a vibration in the core of who I believed myself to be.

This vibration would be the communication link from my individual expression of Consciousness to the One Consciousness. This undetectable vibration was subconscious and strong. Even though I would attempt to send out vibrations of love, I would continue to receive the opposite. This was perplexing. It was not until I stopped thought that I was able to see the fearful, egoic entity. No matter how much willpower you put into creating a life of love, if the subconscious platform from which you exist in life is tainted from the conditioning and paradigms of the past, your physical life will always project back the deepest vibration. Even if your deepest vibration is far from alignment with Source, you will reap that which you sow. In other words, the material world will hand-deliver based upon the frequency from which you vibrate, even if it is negative and you have no awareness of it. That is why alignment is key to a fruitful life. Without knowing what Source knows, you are a pawn for the ego to drag around like a rag doll in a dog's mouth.

Continuing life after stopping thought means to live every second of every day in alignment. This literally means to place alignment first in life before every task, minute-by-minute and day-by-day. With practice, alignment becomes the natural and loving way of life. After stopping thought, life goes on, but it feels like harmony and peace without even trying. The old way of living was based in misalignment to the false self and to the physical world. That way was one of struggle and lack. The new way of living life is through a mental place of ease. Working "hard" may exist to the aligned but will flow from an underlining place of peace and rest.

Chapter Twenty-Two

PERSONAL GUIDE & PROTECTOR

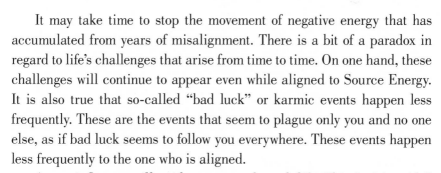

It may take time to stop the movement of negative energy that has accumulated from years of misalignment. There is a bit of a paradox in regard to life's challenges that arise from time to time. On one hand, these challenges will continue to appear even while aligned to Source Energy. It is also true that so-called "bad luck" or karmic events happen less frequently. These are the events that seem to plague only you and no one else, as if bad luck seems to follow you everywhere. These events happen less frequently to the one who is aligned.

A new influence will guide your way through life. This "spirit guide" will watch over you to steer you from the path of the so-called bad luck events. This influence also directs you towards a new destination. The only known denominator is that all is well. I certainly would like to know the next steps for my life, well in advance but that is not the case. All I know is I must follow the promptings of my heart and watch Source Energy pave the road underneath every footstep I take.

Most of my life was consumed with worry prior to alignment. I was really good at making sure I had a safety net or reserve parachute for everything I did. While working a regular job, I would peruse the classifieds, even applying to some in the event that I might be fired. I did this even while being consistently promoted beyond my imagination. This protection was not safeguarding me as much as I thought it was. What it really did was make it difficult to enjoy life. I do believe this particular personality trait of mine is what got me promoted time and time again, but it seemed to be both a blessing and a curse.

I am now able to give that job of "protection" and proactive foresight up to a higher calling. Source Energy already knows what pitfalls lay ahead. More importantly, Source Energy's main job is to nourish the individual just as it nourishes the trees and flowers with the rain and sun. It is nice to leave all the worries, fears, and anxiety to someone else. My new purpose in life is to be the individual and unique expression of the One Consciousness. Life is wonderful in this way.

Chapter Twenty-Three

SHIFTING THROUGH TECHNOLOGY

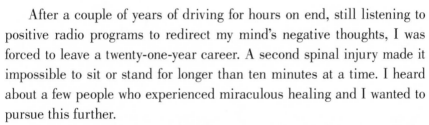

After a couple of years of driving for hours on end, still listening to positive radio programs to redirect my mind's negative thoughts, I was forced to leave a twenty-one-year career. A second spinal injury made it impossible to sit or stand for longer than ten minutes at a time. I heard about a few people who experienced miraculous healing and I wanted to pursue this further.

My first spinal injury occurred in 2005. A spinal discectomy on the L5/S1 would fix that injury and got me back behind the wheel for another eleven years. My surgeons did not recommend I pursue physical therapy as a first course of action for the next injury. The MRI showed a bulging disc pushing on a nerve and they recommended surgery right away.

Electrical shocks would shoot down my right leg and, on occasion, I would collapse onto the ground from the pain. It was serious, but I wanted to press on with the supernatural healing I heard about. I could not walk much farther than ten minutes at first. While walking, I would listen to positive affirmations. I never let my mind go to a negative place. If I was unable to stop worrying about my future, which happened often at first, I would put earbuds in and redirect my mind with something uplifting. I believe this was key to my initial success. At the time, it was hard to see progress. Again, it was as slow as watching the grass grow.

I was also battling an alcohol addiction. This was right after my divorce and losing the close proximity to my two children. The mortgage payments came up short and the credit card bills stacked up. I was facing addiction, financial troubles, relationship troubles, and a physical injury that would all prove to be a battle I would win - eventually. I kept my head in the self-help books and made positive affirmations. I walked in any weather. I remember my sister telling me that she was worried about me being all alone and walking so much. She called me Forrest Gump. I would walk in the ice and snow at a park in Pennsylvania for about thirty minutes at a time. It was excruciatingly painful. The muscle spasms would cramp up through the right buttock muscle and down that leg. I would walk until the spasm would release its tension. Each time I walked, the spasm would start a little later in the walk and it would take more steps to get it to release.

Eventually, I was able to walk farther and farther. By the time I noticed a substantial difference, I was walking twelve miles in a single day just to get the muscle spasm to release. Something was definitely changing for me. It was a combination of mental and physical, plus the belief in a higher power. It took all three. I refused to listen to the part of me that wanted to give up. Eventually, I would kick the alcohol habit, pay off the credit card debt, restore the relationships with both of my children, and make it to the gym to do some light exercise.

Some time had passed, and I was offered one promotion after another until I would eventually land a work-from-home job as a computer geek and spreadsheet nerd. I say that with a bit of humble pride because those things were never my strong suit. While it is obvious that none of the miracles that happened to me were served on a platter without effort, Source Energy, God, or whatever name you prefer, was leading my way. Without faith and hope, I would have been on a much quicker path to the grave and I certainly would not have managed to have hour-long conversations with my daughter from the beaches of the Eastern Shore. My daughter and I lost contact after the divorce, and I was elated to regain that relationship while living at the beach. My son and I were a bit distant, but the communication was there, and I appreciated that.

Through all of this, I learned that I am nothing without Source. I can do nothing without Source. I also learned that with the help of Source, all things are possible. Something vitally more important happened as well. I learned that nothing good comes from acting without being aligned. Alignment means fulfillment. I leaned hard on Source Energy and verbalized words of healing and faith no matter how I felt on the inside or outside. My back would have awful muscle spasms while I was walking. I just kept saying stuff like, "I am healed, and I am whole."

This is where I learned the power of the mind. Left alone, the mind will turn a person into a victim and a slave. Through alignment with Source, one receives wisdom, grace, power, and forgiveness to embody the meaning of a miraculous life. I have learned a lot while on this path, but the greatest lesson is that the world is everything your mind makes it out to be. If you think you cannot do something, you will not. If you are trying, you will forever be trying. Getting past those burdens in my life took developing a new mindset. "Trying" and "should have" became words of the past. I realized that the universe loves so deeply, it wants you to express yourself however you desire. Through alignment, desires are not needs.

I played a game of opposites with my negative emotions. Every time my mind would say something defeatist like, "You will never do this." I would say out loud, the complete opposite. When I was promoted to Site Manager for an under-performing logistics company that was nearly dead last in its division, my mind told me that all I knew was twenty-one years of driving and I possessed very little management skills. I turned that thought around and said out loud, "I am leading the number one site in the division." Eight months later, I did just that. The lesson here is that whatever you verbalize and align your inner energy field with, you will become. Do not forget that your requests in alignment are heard and acted upon immediately, but just as when watching the grass grow, you will need to be patient.

If you are stuck in the "help me, help me" phase, Source will come running to your aid. There is no question about that, but that is where it ends. We must be willing to say the "I am's." You must be willing to repeat, "I am strong," when you are feeling weak, "I am healthy," when you are sick, and so forth. We also need to guard our mind. Do not let negativity survive there. Do not believe its lies. That is the false you. Remember that it is only through alignment that you will be at peace. Do not do what I did and muscle through a spinal injury and back pain because you read it in this book. You are missing the point if you do that. You may be called to do something else. My shoulder and knee injury did not become miraculously healed. You need to be aligned and then go through life as your own individual expression of the same Consciousness from which you came. Your answers are not in this book. Your answers are in your *heart* when it is in alignment with the One Consciousness.

My cell phone was a huge asset in helping me change my thoughts. If I was unable to stop negative thinking, I would listen to anything uplifting. I never let my mind go wandering off to do its own thinking. It was a timer for practicing quieting the mind, it was a source of distraction when the mind wanted to worry, and I downloaded a recording app to record myself. The recording app became instrumental in tweaking this journey to be suited just for me. I was listening to tons of affirmations recorded by others. They all helped a lot, but they were all geared towards someone else. I needed specific affirmations in the areas where I struggled. I once heard that the sweetest sound to a person is the sound of their own name. I figured that maybe the sound of my own voice, saying my own name, while talking about the specific areas I needed improvement in, would be helpful.

It is okay to say affirmations like, "I want to get better at this or that," or "I want to get rid of my back pain," but recognize that the vibrations you are sending out are less than where you want to be. For instance, if I am saying that I am trying, it is a great start, but you will eventually want to get to the point of saying that you are exactly what you are not at the present moment. I started out saying, "Please take away the headaches and make the vomiting go away," when I was trying to quit drinking. Notice the word "trying" in the previous sentence as well as actually affirming that I had a problem by addressing the problem with the words "please take away." That is a good place to start, but to receive a vibration of good health, you must align your own expression of Consciousness with the One Consciousness, know who you really are, and affirm with your own vibration that you are indeed healed, healthy, and whole.

Do not worry if your ego tells you that saying you are strong when you are weak is a lie. If you do not know who you truly are, it will feel like a lie to you. When you are aligned, all things are possible. As with my injured knee and shoulder, I still affirm that I am healthy. Alignment is not about being healed in the physical dimension as much as it is about knowing your true essence. Within alignment is freedom, not in healing. I still record my voice and claim I am healed, but I do not "need" the healing for fulfillment in the way someone living out of the ego "needs" something in the physical dimension. I am already whole and healed on the deepest level and that is where I live my life. Living from alignment means that the earth is a playground, and my body is the earth suit that I am able to use before I return back to the loving arms of the same Consciousness we all are a part of. It means as far as Consciousness is concerned, your existence on earth takes place in the blink of an eye and there is no need to worry.

Chapter Twenty-Four

BREAKING DYSFUNCTIONAL MIND PATTERNS

After getting a glimpse into the peace that passes all understanding, I found myself in another struggle. The habitual mind wanted to return to a busy place of monitoring, judging, labeling, and complaining - all to keep me "safe." Occasionally, I would fall for the trick. My mind would tell me to do anything other than feel peaceful. It would invent things to do. While these tasks were all fine things to do, like laundry or washing the car, they did not need to be done at that present moment. I noticed that I followed the commands of my busy mind right into insomnia and quite possibly insanity years ago.

I saw how this was tiring me out. The old days were filled with busyness and work, all disguised by rationalizing. I was already a responsible person, so the egoic excuse that it is all part of being responsible did not resonate with me anymore. The layers of my false self were slowly being removed. Eventually, after practicing being in this peaceful state, I was able to see myself separately from myself. I was able to see the ego tell me to get up from meditation and do something. Sometimes I would return to the robot-like entity (i.e., the ego) that I seemed to be and would kind of wake up while following its commands. In the middle of leaving the peaceful place of mental rest, I would catch myself two steps away from doing this or that. None of which needed to be done at that moment but knowing this truth would begin to release me from the grips of the ego.

I would stop whatever the mind wanted me to do and return it to a place of rest by focusing on my breathing and the other five senses. I had to be in a high state of awareness - on the lookout. If I did not constantly monitor myself in this way, the ego would sneak in and command me to wear the body out tirelessly in an effort to feed it more empowering energy to keep it alive within me. Through practice, I would leave the grips of the habitual ego as well.

Life cannot be seen for what it truly is until we separate ourselves from it. I was swimming in a pool looking up from the bottom. I was imagining what it would be like to be a fish and see the way the birds fly, people walk by, and children play, but from the perspective of the fish and not knowing how to be a part of that experience. As I read books written by some very spiritual people, I felt a little like a fish might have felt. I would say to myself, "I am here - suffering. How do I get to where there is no suffering?"

This is the dilemma we all face when in the midst of suffering. Imagine you are the fish. Imagine different ways a fish might leave the water. Imagine a hawk catches you, takes you high enough to see the world from a new vantage point, possibly from a place of peace, when suddenly you are dropped back to the old place of confinement, the water. That is much how I felt in the beginning, during the times I suffered greatly. I would taste and feel the peace that passes all understanding, but it was fleeting. Maybe after an accidental glimpse of Heaven from a hawk, the fish is instead pushed ashore by the winds or maybe out of desperate measures to reclaim that destination as more permanent, the fish swims hard to beach itself. I was like that fish, and I imagine many others are too.

Finding peace comes in many ways. There is no wrong way, but once you have seen the light, so to speak, you will either suffer more through seeking, or you will simply attain Heaven from within. There is only more suffering in the seeking. The habitual patterns will emerge from the past and at that moment, the choice is yours - if you are aware enough. It is then that you can take your life back. It is not after the laundry is finished or once the religious or meditative modality has given it to you. You must do the mental work - the hard stuff. You must receive the gift of peace at this moment and at every moment.

You only have that short glimpse of awareness to break the habitual egoic pattern. It does not come later. The moment you choose later, you have chosen to be a slave to your ego. Obviously, if an emergency arises you will want to tend to it immediately. If the laundry does need to be done and you can simply return your mind to alignment with Source for ten minutes before doing the laundry, you have weakened the ego. Procrastinators might use this as a way to strengthen their ego in an effort of laziness. Only you will know if you are deceiving yourself in this manner.

It is best to just "be alert" for as much of your waking moments as possible. I like to refer to my alertness as being atop the watchtower. It is obvious to most that circumstances and the ego go hand-in-hand if you are not paying attention. It may not be as obvious that the habitual thoughts can be just as much an outer form of disruption to alignment as circumstances are. Many of us are aware that challenges come and go. We know that challenges may come to wreak havoc on our stable mindsets.

Thoughts can be just as much a form of disruption to our lives. We recognize through thought that something could be wrong and our alignment with Source is shaken. We might think a fearful thought that takes us off of balance with Source Energy. It is important to note that sometimes our thoughts can be destructive forms of habitual energy patterns. Many times, the thought that feels pressing, imperative, and important, is a habitual thought that will recur time and time again. It likely will not be the same physical thing that its alarm bells are sounding about, but it will be within the habitual time frame. The thought arises to fulfill the mind's need for the chemical substance that is created.

The only way around this is through starving it, so to speak. It is good to know that life will improve exponentially. Well, life does not really improve. I became absorbed in spending every moment in alignment with Source and I improved. Not as a better person but as a better emanation of Consciousness. Instead of losing myself to the slavery of the ego's demands, that I believed in so erroneously, I became forgetful of the old self. I became one with Source. It is a wonderful experience that can never be had at a later point in time. It is best to align at the moment you become aware. Awareness itself is alignment but when this practice is first started, I needed to remind myself to align. You may need to do the same.

My habitual old self was melting away as I used time to deliberately pull me out of time. It was a paradox. The deeper on the journey I progressed, the greater the magnetic pull is to align with Source Energy more and more of the time. It is as if I started hearing a new voice taking the place of the old slave driver. This felt like I was being told, "It is okay. Relax. Good things are coming to you." I did not realize just how remarkable this would be. My energy shifted. Through this awareness, I was able to see just how destructive and damaging the old habitual voice was.

This old voice was supposedly keeping me safe. It never once did that. I began to hear the old voice through alignment with Source. There was no more rationalizing. I heard it for what it was - a scared entity, created by myself as a young child in a desperate attempt to protect myself. I was actually okay with that too. I became okay with everything. There was only life. There is no wrong or right. It just is what it is. With this, came freedom.

I was able to see that I was the destructive pattern in my life. The only enemies were me or the ego and loving myself and the ego for the sake of love will set you free. It is impossible to place blame on anything when aligned with Source. The life that I felt was against me in the past showed me that it is not for or against anyone. The feeling of suffering, loss, and lack, disappeared. I recognized myself - my true self. It was beautiful.

Chapter Twenty-Five
STRUGGLE VS. ALLOW

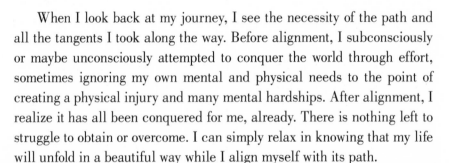

When I look back at my journey, I see the necessity of the path and all the tangents I took along the way. Before alignment, I subconsciously or maybe unconsciously attempted to conquer the world through effort, sometimes ignoring my own mental and physical needs to the point of creating a physical injury and many mental hardships. After alignment, I realize it has all been conquered for me, already. There is nothing left to struggle to obtain or overcome. I can simply relax in knowing that my life will unfold in a beautiful way while I align myself with its path.

People do not know who they are without alignment. I have heard people say, "Be unapologetically you." To the person living from the ego, this creates more havoc as they unapologetically go through life. That statement is absolutely true for both the person aligned with Source and the one who is not, but the world is a much better place as more people become aware of who they truly are. It is only through alignment that who we are is a blessing to the world. When we realize all other humans are a reflection of ourselves, we have no enemies and do not live in fear. We do not live to gain or strive to build a safe place in this world. All is already gained. The world is already safe. Peace, security, and abundance of all things are already yours.

Now that I comfortably realize the infinite Source from which I am an emanation of, I need nothing. What the person living from the false, egoic self may not realize about "needing nothing" is the transference of the specific things that are "needed." To the person living through misalignment, "needed" items are three dimensional and material objects of the world. The physical world "needs" to be a certain way in order to be happy, stress free, and secure. "Needed" things, to the person living aligned, do not exist, other than the obvious basics like food and water. The "need" for anything to be different from the way it currently is, does not exist for the person who is aligned. Yes, it is true that I would like for some things to be different, but I am complete and lacking nothing, no matter what the world does around me.

The whole idea of what is "needed" changes when you become aligned. Your inner joy and gratitude for simply being alive supersedes any material objects. I have zero "needs" in order to feel complete. To the person who is not aligned, something is "needed" to attain inner peace or happiness which is always temporary when gotten through the act of "needing" and misalignment. It is almost like misalignment is a fish "needing" water to breathe but once aligned, the fish realizes that the water was an illusion. After alignment, the fish sees something it was not able to see prior to alignment. The fish now sees that the "need" for water was an illusion. This is why it is so hard to explain alignment to someone living from their false self. It makes absolutely no sense to that person.

Sometimes the attempts to explain alignment just muddy the water. The more a person dives into explanations, the more holes that show up in the theory. (I'll stop using water analogies now). The reason is because a non-aligned person uses a method of truth, deductive reasoning, and the finite, clever-thinking mind to analyze the inconceivable or unexplainable. How do you describe something that cannot be named or even completely understood with the conceptual mind? It cannot be done. That is why it is so important to give the "student" a license to veer off course at any time to pursue the inner calling that feels more like home to them. It is through this individual self-discovery that one will find alignment and the peace that passes all understanding.

Another hurdle you may face is the feeling that you are not important enough to enter a mental place where the One Consciousness exists. Conversely, you may think you are already connected when you indeed are not. It is egoic to think less than yourself as well as more than yourself. You must come boldly to the throne but as a "nobody." You cannot bring your resume with you into a meditation of alignment, nor can you bring your depressed self. Both are egoic ways of identifying with the false self. I certainly was skeptical that time spent devoid of thought would produce inner peace. Even though I was stubborn at first and did not believe it, I am still surprised when someone tells me he/she is unable to take two minutes to practice no thought.

Why would a person suffering from anxiety, depression and other negative emotions continue to suffer when they know the way to relief is through practicing quieting the mind for just two minutes at a time? Because they either do not believe it, or they do not want to stop feeling like a victim. Both of those cases were true in my circumstance. I did not realize just how mentally unwell I was until I aligned myself with Source. Being under the influence of the false self is destructive. Just like when a person is deceived into thinking they like the substance they are addicted to, I was misguided in the suffering. I did not know it then, but I was choosing to be a victim while suffering from anxiety. I used to think I loved the taste of chewing tobacco. When I quit, I realized I was being played a fool by the addiction to it. My brain thought it liked it. In the same way, I was choosing to suffer from anxiety all the while my brain's addiction to the suffering was blaming something else.

While in California with my daughter, Hannah, she mentioned to me that she could feel the sincerity inside me for the first time. This was when I was expressing my love and apologies to her for my mistakes. She said, "I know Dad. I can feel that you are different." When I hug my son, Nick, I feel like I am actually giving and sending love. Before my alignment, I was empty inside. I "needed" certain things in order to feel whole and complete. After alignment, I feel like I am a "giver" of good vibrations and energy. Before alignment, I had no idea how incomplete of a foundation I was living my life from. Emptiness used to be a void I tried to fill through worldly events, achievements, and so forth, but I had no idea. I thought I was happy, but deep down I felt like something was not quite right.

It is only when the need for something becomes so debilitating, that we have lost our way. Another way to explain this is if we settle, compromise, or throw away our morals to gain something, we are probably searching for something to fill a void within. When I think back to the time I spent the evening with a woman simply to feel affection, I am relieved my actions as an aligned person will no longer be initiated from a mental place of lack. That is an example of living from the false self. Through my neediness, I was hurting others. I operated from a place of mental insufficiencies. I now pursue relationships as a giver, not a taker. I am already fulfilled, and I do not need affection to feel good. I like affection. I want affection. I appreciate affection when I get it, but I do not need it to be complete and I certainly will not use someone to receive it.

Some people take on careers and status to fill an inner void before becoming aligned. Some drink alcohol to turn off the overactive mind because they cannot shut it down themselves. This also stems from a mental place of scarcity and fear. If you quiet the mind through alignment, you might be afraid that you will miss something. Erroneously, you might assume your overactive mind protects your children and through persistent worry, you will uncover something that is missing. It is all false. Stopping thought allows the One Consciousness that created you to align with your own unique expression of the One Consciousness. The thinking, clever mind can follow instructions and even invent things, but the infinite wisdom that created the world, stars, and moons, knows way more about protecting your children than you could ever imagine. Tapping into the knowledge of the creator is the way.

Living a life from the false self is based on living from an inner void based in fear and lack. Living this way, you "take" from the world for your own satisfaction and gain. Many who are living this way, do not know it and they certainly do not know there is an easier way to live life. It still amazes me that many people, including myself years ago, have a winning lottery ticket and never know it. This ticket is your voucher to inner wholeness, completeness, and fulfillment. I had everything I ever needed and did not know it. That is just amazing. It is also true that the world changes when you look at it differently. That has been the case for me. The world is a much more pleasant place than I once perceived.

You cannot get it wrong when you are aligned. By being aligned you let the One Consciousness handle everything and your purpose is to allow life to unfold through you while being in complete harmony and peace. Life's curve balls and challenges will come. There will be times when you are not happy, even times when you are sad, but the core foundation from which you rest all of your being on, is the rock of the peace that comes from the One Consciousness. This deep connection will give you the strength to ride through those valleys in life with peace. This deep connection will also allow you to be a conscious "giver" by choice in life rather than an unconscious "taker" through fear and lack. All of this can be yours if you are willing. I was forced to surrender my egoic ways. My physical ailments, financial hardships, and relationship difficulties tag-teamed me into surrender. As the mixed martial arts saying goes, "I tapped out." I wanted no more of life's suffering. Peace can be attained without going through all of that. You can break the habitual patterns through practicing two minutes of no thought and find for yourself the peace that passes all understanding.

After years of suffering, I finally asked myself how long have I been dealing with the same questions, struggles, and emotional pain? Why have I not come up with an answer yet? Are you halfway through your lifespan on earth? Are you still struggling and suffering? Are you ready to try something new or do you need to suffer more? When a person has bought into the idea of the types of physical reality defined by Newtonian-type laws, they are unwilling to try something outside the box. Is this you? If you knew for certain that freedom could be found by shifting your thoughts, would you take two minutes to quiet your mind? Most people are unable to believe this for a myriad of reasons. One reason is because the cause of their trouble has shifted. No longer can they "blame" their parents, school, or abuse for their suffering.

Of course, there is no blame once alignment occurs, but to the false self, rejecting the idea that others are not to blame, is ridiculous. Also, just as ludicrous is the idea that they themselves can choose peace right now. Why? Because if they have the choice to choose peace right now and have always had the choice to choose peace, it will mean their entire life was wasted and lived in suffering for no reason at all. Of course, when aligned, there is no blame, guilt, shame, fear, or loss of any kind. These are the reasons the person living from the false self is not willing to make the shift of consciousness through alignment. To do so takes away their "importance." Again, through alignment, personal importance in the way the ego sees it, does not exist. The ego needs the hierarchy and structure of accomplishments and/or failures. When living aligned, we do not need to broadcast the importance of our new car on social media. Why? Because once aligned, you are already secure in the knowledge that you are an emanation of the One Consciousness. There is no need to compare, compete, or judge and label. Everything is already known.

As a creature living from the false self, we created the egoic suffering in an attempt to regain something we did not know we already had. Through alignment to Source we see the folly of living through the eyes of the ego. The ego refuses to quiet the thinking mind and makes millions of excuses for years and years. How can a human be duped time and time again, over and over? How are humans able to lay in the mess they have created for their entire lifespan and never come to see that they indeed caused the mess? How can a human deeply entangled in suicidal depression, chronic anxiety, or even mild suffering all of their lives not know that the doorway to freedom is just a shift in consciousness away? It is because humans wholeheartedly believe in the foolishness of their ways as factual, and they will suffer all the way to their grave to prove it.

I chose to live the last half of my life through alignment to Source Energy, even though I did not believe one word of the concept at first. Why? Because of two reasons. The first was because I wanted change, desperately. The second was because something deep within me knew it to be true. I actually set out in life not knowing any of this stuff would work. I kept trying the no thought concept until a tiny gap of no thought was noticed. After that, I was hooked. Peace waits for all who are willing to drop what they think they know for something they know nothing about. Just two minutes at a time opened the door to peace on earth for me. You do not have to wait until tonight to try it. You do not have to take a vacation to start the process. All you have to do is to align at every second of every day and the new habit will form.

Trusting in yourself that the connection made to the One Consciousness will bring wisdom and peace, is difficult for many people. People are deeply tied to their beliefs. So much so that they will die before trying something else. I think about some I know who continue to suffer from anxiety, depression, and/or fear. Still to this day, one of these people will come to me with their stressful life's moments and ask for relief. I ask, "How many times did you practice no thought today? Yesterday? Even though they have excuses not to practice the stillness of no thought, I know they still need to suffer more before they will give it a try. That is all that can be said. People who do not practice no thought and are suffering, have not suffered enough. Why? Because some people, like myself, need to be crippled and on their knees before they will try something else. How much more suffering do you need? It is my hope that some will stop the suffering and begin to practice the quiet place of no thought. That is why I have written this book. I have great empathy and compassion for those suffering. I, too, was once part of the dysfunctional thoughts created by the mind.

The peace that passes all understanding is sweet. It is calm. It is better than being on vacation. It is more than euphoric bliss. It is deep, lasting, and true. It is unbelievable how the presence of God is a million times better than any worldly event. It is no wonder the lost search the world for what they are missing. They have no idea what they are missing, so they search the world. What else is there to do from the human mental position? At every given second of every given day, you have a choice to align or stay stuck.

I remember a time when I was in the middle of cleaning up the mess, I called my life. I was working in Winchester, Virginia. I had horrible back pain, an enormous amount of money on credit cards after my divorce, and I was pretty much a complete mess in the way in which the physical world would classify me. The guys at work knew me as "Mr. Positive." Even though on the inside I was afraid, I followed all the teachings of the influential spiritual leaders. When I would get back to my apartment at the end of the day, which was riddled with mold and bugs, I would throw all my energy into imagining a new life for myself. It was hard, but I stayed positive. The guys at work would ask me how I stayed so positive. I always said, "All that is left for me to do is to hit home runs." When you have been on the bottom and do not ever want to go back, there is just one thing to do. Stop listening to your egoic self. The next few years were years of great physical and mental growth. My spirit rejoiced as the ego was silenced.

The struggle is with dropping the ego. Allowing abundance to unfold is really hard to understand with the false mind. It is just better to align and allow. Do not question anything. A friend of mine felt that you must discover why and how the past was the way it was before moving on in life. To this person it was very important to understand why anxiety and depression existed. She also felt that negative emotions needed to be dealt with, otherwise you would be suppressing emotions, which we all know is unhealthy. One day, while meditating together, this person experienced a glimpse of the peace that passes all understanding. I asked, "Did you need to figure out why the past was the way it was or where the anxiety came from in order to feel that sense of peace while meditating?" She answered, "No." I asked, "Did you need to suppress negative emotions to feel eternal peace?" Again, the answer was no. Right there was a glimpse into Heaven. It proved that you can choose peace. With practice, you can take this peaceful mindset into the chaotic world and feel the peace that passes all understanding.

When aligned, you will no longer compete with another, nor will you feel superior or inferior. Notice your own emotions when you recognize another person is ahead or behind you in worldly status. Notice your inner emotions as you go about your day. Does another person upset you? Does another person seem pitiful to you? Do you feel jealousy? These are all normal emotions that we all have from time to time. When aligned, we feel an emotion and then make internal changes to adjust ourselves back to an emotion of love and acceptance. Some people living from the false self will feel something like jealousy, anger, or resentment, and wish that the situation was changed. When aligned, the person feeling negative emotions recognizes the emotions as friendly signs that read, "You have lost your way. Peace is over here." The aligned person will make an inner change. Remember, Source created everything, including the person you feel angry or jealous towards, and you are an emanation of Source. The problem is not with the other person. The problem is with your perception. When aligned, perception comes from a neutral area of love and acceptance of all things. Whatever that person has done or said that stirred up negative emotions in you, is actually an emotional mirror image of yourself. Clean up your own vibration and the world will begin to reflect back to you a new reality.

Let's cover the idea about the world reflecting back to you your own image. The reflection is not an exact copy of the physical dimension. If an angry man shows up in your life scenario it could be a reflection of your inner vibration. What? You are not an angry person, you are wondering? There is much to unpack here. All negative emotions have a root cause in fear. What is the main human and egoic position? Fear. The ego is in constant fear. An angry person is acting out of fear. So is an anxious person. The depressed person is acting in fear also. I was depressed at one time because I did not feel like life was fair, and that I did not measure up. In that example, I feared that I was missing something. Look around you. Notice the circumstances. It is not a perfect rule of thumb to follow, but you will know if this explanation works for you or not. Obviously, there are counselors working with individuals that do not mirror the same. I make these points to help you to look into your own life. I realize not all of this is true for everyone.

You will notice sweeter and more loving people as you become more loving. Watch your inner self closely. Notice if you have a sense of rushing. I have been divorced for quite some time. On occasion, I feel like I should have a partner by now. When aligned I feel whole, even in the absence of a partner. All things that come and go while aligned are blessings. If I rush, I will be out of alignment and I will be creating a relationship from a place of lack through the false and needy self. That relationship will not be sustainable. I will create more of the same relationships as I did in the past. The one who is aligned will want the peace that comes with trust more than anything the world has to offer. In time, all things will come to the one who is aligned.

Pretend for a moment the vibrations inside of you are like a jar filled with yellow and blue marbles. Pretend the blue marbles are negative energy that consists of everything from severe anxiety to low-level uneasiness. The yellow marbles are love. You and I both want to remove all the blue marbles that stand for negative energy and replace them with yellow marbles that stand for love. No one will argue with that. What people may not know is that negative energy comes in subtle forms. One subtle negative energy form is describing the bad parts of your day in a way that encourages negative energy growth. Only you will know if there is a rise in negative energy within you or if you are stating facts about the day. Stating facts could be like filling a jar with yellow marbles. Complaining is filling the jar with blue marbles. The problem is that many have jars filled with blue marbles and they still want to hold onto them.

How much guilt is appropriate after doing something bad? Is guilt a useful tool for keeping you from doing bad things? Guilt is an emotion created by the ego that slaps negativity on top of negativity. Guilt is a toxic negative energy. Let's say you made a small mistake. How much time is needed to spend feeling guilty before you have fully paid for the offense? How about a large mistake? How much time spent in guilt is necessary? If you think any time spent feeling guilt is okay, you are wrong. Guilt is like a toxic drink. Every time guilt is felt deeply, you are taking a sip of poison. To notice guilt and let it pass through you is to practice awareness. There is nothing wrong with noticing the guilt and letting it go. Emotions come and go, but to become immobilized from guilt is like drinking poison. Make sure you are filling up your jar with loving, yellow marbles.

If you are feeling negative emotions like anxiety, you may have too many blue marbles in your jar. You may need to forget about figuring out why the anxiety is there for the time being. You might want to start loading up on the loving, yellow marbles no matter what, until you tip the balance, and the anxiety begins to fade. Doing so will help your alignment and get the ball rolling in a healthier direction for you. You need to look at your body like that jar of marbles and realize that harboring any negativity, whether it is justified or not, still creates stress in your body that leads to some form of illness. It does not matter who, why, how, or when. You are deliberately hurting yourself by doing so.

When my daughter was not talking to me, I knew not to let negative energy form inside of me. A short time after I moved to Las Vegas to be closer to her and my son, she moved to Maine. We restored our relationship prior to her leaving. If I would have been upset that she moved to Maine just as I moved out west, I would be sending negative energy through my body and to the world. I may have sent that negative energy off to the grocery store clerk or the negative energy could have come back to me in some other form of loss or pain. Living like the inside of your body needs only the yellow marbles, allows for freedom. Most importantly it allows others to be free to be their imperfect selves. All is love at that point.

Check your mental state for grudges, resentment, jealousy, pride, and so forth. Acts of self-love are when we throw away the blue marbles that have other people's names on them. Even if something is their fault. Why? Because we love ourselves too much to carry around negative energy, even if we were deliberately hurt by another. The same goes for your own thoughts and actions. Are you upset or worried about something you did or did not do? If so, you are stacking up blue marbles. Again, it is okay to feel upset. It is not okay for the emotion to immobilize you. Negative energy is negative energy. It does not matter why, who, or how. Forgiveness is for you. When you forgive, you will be forgiven as well. Be on the "watch tower" as I call it. Monitor the inner emotions. Love yourself unconditionally no matter what unfolds. If you screw up, remember the ego will sneak in through the back door with a guilt trip. Remember, negative emotions are negative emotions. A guilt trip is another form of egoic suppression that will keep you stuck. You must love yourself unconditionally so that the world can do the same for you. The world is the mirror reflection of yourself. The people you encounter, whether good or bad, are teaching you about you. It is not about them. The feelings you have towards another are just what you see in them that is also in you.

If you are not happy with your life and there seems to be a lot of negativity, take a self-check of your own inner emotions. Do not worry if you have created a mess in your life and you just figured it out. All is well. Take this moment to meditate and send love to every cell in your body. Remember what you have learned so far. To feel guilty is to miss the mark. Always send love. Always have a self-check on your emotions and always send love. Realize and understand that to be misaligned is kind of like being sick or having a broken bone. Alignment is the healed self. Everything comes to light when aligned. Peace within is felt. Nothing is missing. Security and love are yours. Abundance is yours. Take everything you once carried on your back and drop it. Place it on the ground, walk away, and leave it there. Where you are going, you will not need anything, especially not the burdens you have been carrying for so long.

I spent the first half of my life not aligned. I did not know it then, but I was chasing material objects to fill an inner void. My physical life was filled with examples of exactly that. My marriage, house, job, vehicle, and so on were all manifestations of completeness on the outside and emptiness on the inside. It was not until after alignment to Source that my relationships with my two kids began to strengthen on the deepest level of true love. I mentioned earlier that my daughter told me that she could feel just how genuine I am now. We do not know what we do not know and that is okay. Before alignment, I was empty on the inside. The world around me was built on emptiness, which of course is an easy structure to destroy when life gets rough. The farm life we lived was beautiful on the outside. I am not married now but my then-wife drove a Ford, Eddie Bauer edition truck with hand stitched leather seats. The car was shiny, but the relationship was not. My inground pool was full of crystal-clear water, but I was completely empty on the inside. Nearly everything in the physical realm was an exact replica of how I felt. I needed to put up a facade on the outside to cover up the void on the inside.

The reason I tell you this is because I want to be an example of how one can be fulfilled on the inside through alignment. I did not give up the fancy horse farm or humble myself by taking less money in my career because I wanted to become spiritually aligned. I was forced to make these changes, but through all of it, I have adopted what I think is a sense of value to the human experience called life. I have learned the greatest lesson there is. That is love. You cannot love your friends, the world, or anything, for that matter, unless you first unconditionally love yourself and this only happens through alignment. As long as we are living from the ignorance of the false, egoic self, we are unknowingly creating havoc for ourselves, family, friends, strangers, and the earth. The best way to clean up this messy world we live in is to clean up our own ignorance.

You can hate the neighbor that wronged you. You can insult the person with purple hair. You can mock, fear, be prideful, or take revenge, but the finger always points back at you. The emotions you feel about others, your own thoughts, and situations are just pointers reminding you to align. The further we get from alignment, the harsher the physical becomes. Depression, anxiety, worry, and insomnia will creep back into our lives as pointers to return to Source Energy. You do not have to lose your health, marriage, sleep, finances, or relationships through suffering as I did. You can choose peace now by practicing alignment starting with just two minutes at a time.

There is no doubt that you will create all the same garbage in your life if you have not aligned with Source. Are you starting over? New job? New relationships? New house? One clear sign that you will manifest more of the same dysfunction in your life is if you are "seeking" or "needing" change to fill an inner void. If your self-talk is something based in lack due to unpleasant circumstances, you are emitting a vibration of lack even though your outer efforts are to strive to achieve something better. Be careful about how you "start over." Through alignment one will send a vibration of completeness and receive just that.

If you are on the path to alignment, it just means you are aware of the false self. The "efforting" part of alignment comes by breaking the habitual patterns that used to steer your life into the gutter. Rest assured, when aligned, Source will be there every step of the way. You can relax in the peace that passes all understanding, even if you have only aligned yourself for just a nanosecond. Once you have seen the light, the light is always turned on for guidance, but you must make the mental effort to stop the habitual thoughts. That is the only effort you will need to make and taking that action the moment of your awareness is essential. Source will guide your steps and tell you when to take the next appropriate action.

Now when I think about "wanting" something, it is completely different from the "neediness" I used to feel. The only thing I want is alignment. It is a beautiful state of mind to traverse life. I already feel complete. I am not worried about anything. I do not need to have my life in perfect order. I trust that life will bring me the challenges I need for growth, the blessings of God, and the peace to rest in. Everything else is fleeting anyway. More money or a better job will not bring me security until I have found security within myself. My bucket list starts first with being aligned to Source. After that, I will make my way through life experiencing adventure and relationships as the blessings they were designed to be.

Here is a way to look at the life energy that is peering through your own eyes at this very moment. Imagine a puppet show. You know someone is behind the wall holding a puppet in his/her hand. The voice, laughter, and personality come from the puppeteer. Imagine that you have gone to this puppet show for years and the personality, laughter, and voice comes from a woman with a jovial attitude. You are accustomed to the creator of this puppet behaving a certain way. The gestures, voice, and laughter are very specific and during the puppet show the audience senses the life of the puppet. After the show, you see the puppet lying lifeless on a shelf. It is empty and void of the unique personality that made it entertaining.

I apologize in advance for what I am about to say but I promise I will make a good point. A human body lying lifeless in a casket at a funeral is less than ten percent of who that person truly was. Metaphorically speaking, the creator of the universe took the hand of life out of the body lying in the casket. When we look at a lifeless body, we know beyond a shadow of a doubt, that the life energy we once knew has left us with nearly nothing. The body is all that remains. The body is nearly nothing without the life energy behind it. The life energy that fills the body is the real you. You are not your name, status, or any other label. The real you is the life force that moves inside the body.

Imagine a table with a chocolate cupcake and a rock lying on it. You get to choose which one to take home with you. If your brain was connected to a medical device, you would see exactly where the electrical signal originates in the brain as it sends a signal to one of your hands to pick up your selection. However, science cannot show the "who" that decided between the two choices. The "who" that made the selection is the energy force that resides inside of you. It is the energy force that leaves the body when it dies.

Making a connection to this life-giving source of energy, the One Consciousness, is considered complicated from the mind of the egoic, false self. Connecting to this energy source is simply considered absurd to many people and so they do not even try. I know people that say to me, "I do not have time, or I will try one day." People are so connected to the false self in the physical world that they cannot fathom something that cannot be measured, weighed, or seen. This is no different than the wind that gently pushes leaves from the tall trees or the unseen Source Energy that makes sure you blink your eyes all day long. Deep underneath the layers of who you think you are (i.e., your name, birth date, skin color, career status, rich, poor, privileged, abandoned, etcetera) is the real you. It is the "you" that survives the body's death lying lifeless in a casket. This energy source is the eternal you that never dies, cannot be hurt, has an abundance of all things, and is free. By practicing quieting the mind just two minutes a day, you can begin to know your true self once again.

I do not quite know how to explain the feelings of peace that I feel now. It is like nothing I have ever felt before. As I sit on my back porch and watch the sun begin to set on the palm trees, I know this is where I want to be. If this were my last day on earth, I would want this to be the feeling I would have for the entire day. Sitting here, taking in all the sounds, sights, and smells is wonderful. There is no need for anything else. I do not ever want this feeling to leave me, and so I practice no thought nearly one hundred percent of my days now. While at home in the quiet setting of my back porch it is easy to be still, attentive, and consciously aware of

God. I also practice this while on my Zoom calls for work. The stress level I used to feel during work calls is nonexistent now. Driving, talking with my neighbors, and even exercising can all be done while staying aligned. I still have challenges that arise, unexpected financial setbacks, and so forth but I am able to ask myself, "How much of this will I bring to my grave when I die?" Exactly none is my answer and so why carry that stress around? I have made a couple of big mistakes in my work that would have devastated the old me. For a moment I feel a little upset, I learn from it, and laugh at just how much importance I used to place on the illusion of worldly "stuff." I do not even know who the old me was.

I think about the guy I used to be and wonder how I ever confused and combined the words care, worry, and importance. I used to think that to "care" meant to worry or feel guilty. I also used to think that if I did not feel bad, that meant I did not care. I thought that if something was important, I should feel stressed over it. To take it a step further, when I mentally decided not to "care," that meant that I decided not to "worry." The false self thought that not caring about something meant that I would not stress over it. Therein lies the unseen issue of the person living from the false self. The attachment of the word worry to the word care. It is much like the mistake of attaching the word care to the word guilt. As if feeling guilty means that one cares. It is totally possible to care about your children and not worry about them. In fact, it is highly important to care about your children and not worry about them. Why? Because of two reasons. The first reason can be found in the physical realm. Children learn by example, and they will eventually acquire this habit and worry or stress over things in which they have no control. The second reason lies in the conscious realm. Your children will pick up the vibrations you emit. They will learn a pattern of behavior from their parents on the subconscious level and not have any clue how it got there or that it is even an erroneous psychological behavior.

This is why alignment to Source is so important. Without being able to "erase" the dysfunctional and undetectable patterns, you will continue to use your "broken" mind to search for an answer. A person's anxiety, fear, worry, depression, and insomnia could stem from an illusion and to tell you the truth, they do. Here is another example to show how this works. Imagine you are born with rose colored contacts. This is a mysterious film covering your eyes that appears clear to others when they look into your eyes. When you look out into the world, you see everything shaded a bit red. This is similar to what happens when suffering from anxiety. When I looked out into the world, a subconscious emotion was stirred up called anxiety. Just as if I was looking through those rose-colored contacts and saw red. Everyone around me would see me and say, "I see green grass. How could you see red grass?" Twelve people could be saying, "We all see a different color than you do, Rob." This is the same for someone suffering from anxiety. Everyone around me was able to participate and enjoy life, but when I went out into life a mental filter distorted what I "emotionally" saw, and I became scared and frightened. This fear in me was undetectable to others. I did not even know what I was afraid of. All I knew was that I felt good and safe under certain "conditions" and that is where I wanted to be.

After alignment, I have switched out my safety zone of "certain conditions" for a new safety zone comprised of a mental state of mind that has been unveiled to me. The peace that passes all understanding is in us all, but it is completely covered up by the false, egoic self. When aligned, we remove the false self and know our true essence. The only so-called practice is breaking the habit of returning to the illusion of fear. Imagine if your whole life you wore those rose-colored contact lenses. It would take quite a while to believe that a tree really is green if you have spent the first forty years of your life seeing it as a different color. Now attach the human emotion of anxiety to it. It is not just a physical color that you would have to overcome, but also a highly charged emotion that stirs up the fight-or-flight chemicals of fear and possibly death. It takes quite a while to break the habit of feeling anxious, but I am living proof that it can be done. As a matter of fact, I deliberately have to drop the illusion of anxiety from time to time. Anxiety is not a debilitating threat to my existence in the way it once was. I no longer lose days, weeks, or even months waiting for the feelings of fear to leave my body. Anxiety is actually now a friend to me. When it arises, I know I have left the connection to Source Energy, and I simply drop the illusion.

Chapter Twenty-Six

INSANITY

Deepak Chopra said, "Fear is the memory of pain. Addiction is the memory of pleasure. Freedom is beyond both." I would also add that fear, pleasure, and freedom are just erroneous thoughts of comparisons that our mind makes while outside of alignment. The other day a technical glitch allowed for an automatic credit card payment to be missed and immediately my mind jumped into a realm I have not lived in for quite some time. After falling peacefully to sleep, I was awoken by the chatter of my racing mind just two hours after closing my eyes. All sorts of thoughts were racing through my mind as I was unaware that I had slipped back into the fearful, egoic state.

As I lay in bed, I realized that I was overtaken by fearful thoughts of the credit card error and the mess that lay in front of me to clean up. Neither warranted concern at two o'clock in the morning. A few years ago, I may have entertained those thoughts all night long and into the next day. I might have believed that the thoughts were important enough to feel stressed and concerning enough to steal my precious sleep. It is only through alignment that I realized a good night's sleep, despite worldly challenges, is important and necessary. A good night's sleep is more necessary than paying attention to credit card concerns.

While lying in bed I brought my attention back to my body. I used the energy of my racing mind and focused on breathing and alignment. Soon I drifted off to sleep, but it would not be for long. Again, I woke with a racing mind and did the same steps to fall asleep a second time. I repeated this three times before my incessant mind finally receded. It was not a perfect night of sleep, but I gave no power to fear, anxiety, and worry. I stayed at peace. No one is immune to life's challenges and my mind exaggerated them that night. Just as Chopra believes, my fear was indeed directly linked to the memory of my pain. Facing our challenges head on through alignment will always bring us back to a state of peace.

Somehow people have turned anxiety, fear, and worry into a credible and necessary part of handling life's challenges. This does not need to be a part of our daily life. In fact, it should not be. We have a choice to live life in such a way that good sleep and a trust for life can actually be what guides our existence. We can actually live life from a place of mental rest and peace, but many need to know how to get there or even that it is attainable.

Problems are always better solved when we are well rested and in a mental state of peace. It seems easier to solve other people's problems because we are not personally invested. We have not lost sleep over someone else's dilemmas and therefore, we have the ability to think clearly. Our own problems present the most challenges because of the way we choose to mentally process them. We create the idea that our difficulties are of greater concern than someone else's troubles. Many times, we create rational lies (i.e., rationalize) for reasons to stay in this mental state of fear or anxiety.

As I was sitting on my back porch writing this, I realized people have an approach to life that is close to insanity. We sometimes do the same thing over and over and expect a different result. That could very well be the definition of insanity, or at least Einstein may have said so. As I was writing, a fly landed on my cheek. I swished it away and it came back. This happened over and over. The fly was not coming back to annoy me. It was simply being a pesky fly. If I were to get upset and bat the fly with a stick in a frenzy and bruise my skin, you would say I was a little bit crazy, but that is exactly what we do with life's problems. The fly will not stop coming and life's challenges will not either. When will we realize that life is not going to stop throwing challenges at us? When will we stop the insanity of beating it with a stick?

Chapter Twenty-Seven

NEW BOUNDARIES & NEW FREEDOMS

Alignment gives a person healthy boundaries. Boundaries are specific to the individual. Parents, societal rules, the government, friends, religion, and so on have good intentions and do a decent job of steering a young person in the right direction. They all have one common downside. The rules and boundaries are not specific to the individual. They are all well-meaning sources of information, but if a person is not aligned, suffering may occur as a result of living within a boundary that is not meant for him/her. I am not talking about the obvious boundaries like hurting another person. When aligned, any act of violence is something you would not want to do.

From the perspective of the ego, rules such as, do not kill another human being, are needed. When aligned, those rules are already inherently true for the individual. When aligned, a person is pure love and to do anything outside of love, such as an act of violence, would mean that they are actually *not* aligned. With that said, a person that has the boundaries and rules, that are based in conditioning and paradigms, removed from them will be much like a fish that has been given lungs and legs to surface from the water and try out life from a whole new vantage point. For me, I was no longer the "poor little Robbie" I heard so often growing up. To the youngster growing up, even words said without bad intentions, can easily slip deep inside the mind.

When aligned, conditioning from the past is removed. It is a beautiful thing. Even a person's beliefs about their positive qualities can be uprooted. Sometimes we are conditioned to think we love doing something simply because we received more praise as a youngster when we did it. If love was conditional as a kid and receiving accolades from following the orders of others was done to receive some type of love and attention, that person may continue the trend of pleasing others as an adult. Continuing to do the thing that once upon a time brought the feeling of love and not knowing why they feel empty inside, can be a great source of confusion. Sometimes people do things simply because they have always done them that way.

Living aligned allows a person to see that a physical and tangible act of accomplishing anything in this world with the hopes that it will bring them fulfillment is a complete lie. The person living aligned with Source Energy is complete and fulfilled already. It is from this new vantage point that you see the material possessions of the world, and your role in the world, totally different from the egoic and false self. It is through alignment that the old, conditioned self - full of paradigms - is seen for what it really is. Every single person on the planet is an individual and unique expression of the One Consciousness. This One Consciousness is in everything and is the commonality between everything. Through alignment one knows this deeply.

The invisible boundaries of the conditioned self are removed. Mental burdens are carried away like a balloon released and heading for the clouds. The labels and judgments that defined you in the past do not exist anymore. You are whole and healed. You are not just worthy of all good things, but your existence is of all good things. The 65,000 habitual thoughts in your head that have led you down the same path of your life over and over, cease to exist. You are not that voice in your head. You are part of the One Consciousness. You *are* Consciousness.

New boundaries are formed. You learn to love yourself through inner alignment and emotions. One learns that keeping the vibration of love is more important than having to be right. You listen to your body's emotions. If "being right" in a heated debate causes discord within the body, it becomes more important to let the physical and material world go while you stay aligned with peace. The outer world becomes a place to practice balancing harmony within. The outer world is no longer a place to seek fulfillment. One is already fulfilled, and it is more important to stay aligned than anything else.

The only importance is keeping harmony inside. In this way, harmony is the vibration extended to all. You become the light. Seemingly selfish to a person living from the false self, a person deeply aligned has no other intentions other than to stay at rest and peace, even in the midst of a chaotic world. Our inner alignment guides us throughout the day, bringing peace to every situation and leaving the situations that are not receptive to receiving peace. No exceptions. Unconditional love means that you will love yourself despite what worldly conditions are going on. Remember, love of self as the aligned person does not mean, "I worked hard today so I deserve a pizza." That is an example of trying to receive from the world what you already have inside yourself. An aligned person would say, "Someone stole the catalytic converter from my vehicle. I love myself enough to feel good at this moment." Yes, it is okay to be upset about things such as this, but it is not okay to bring on high blood pressure and a heart attack. The idea is to treat yourself to healthy emotions, no matter what happens in the world and allow the negative emotions to pass right through you. That is true love. If you can do that with yourself, you will be able to love others without them needing to be or do something different. Love comes in the form of acceptance, but also while staying at peace.

In a world that is filled with advice - should do and should not do - understanding which direction to take will seem daunting if you are not aligned. Everyone will have good, well-meaning advice for you. Choices that are thought to be unmistakably correct are not always correct for the individual. It is not always good to default to a statistically correct choice when you do not know what you want to do. Bouncing ideas off of your aligned emotional radar screen is best. When aligned, notice the emotional responses inside your body when thinking about a decision. Again, one of two things will happen when something does not resonate while aligned. The thought you are having is not in alignment, or the decision is not in alignment. We carry with us emotions tied to thoughts. If in your past an experience caused pain, the thought is now linked to the pain. This is why we see people who grew up during a war or recession continuing to act in ways they did fifty years ago. They might still be stocking up on a week's supply of food or pinching every penny when there is no need. When aligned, it is not only easy to see our own conditioning from the past, but we are able to change the habit.

When faced with a billion choices in life and no real sense of direction, get aligned. It clears the muddy waters. It allows you to make necessary decisions for your life even while being misunderstood by others. Countless paradigms are removed. Time becomes your friend, not your enemy. Peace fills the mind. Just as effortless as the leaf that is blown in the soft breeze to its new destination, so too will you be lovingly nudged to take the effortless ride called life. There is no more swimming upstream with effort and struggle like the salmon does to lay its eggs. Life will become effortless. You become a blessing in the movement of life.

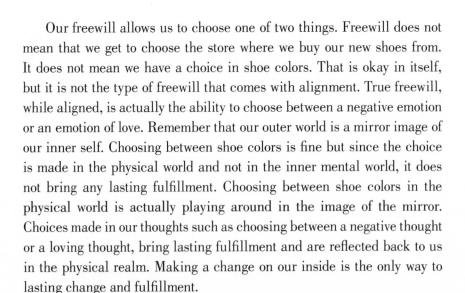

Chapter Twenty-Eight
THE CHOICE

Our freewill allows us to choose one of two things. Freewill does not mean that we get to choose the store where we buy our new shoes from. It does not mean we have a choice in shoe colors. That is okay in itself, but it is not the type of freewill that comes with alignment. True freewill, while aligned, is actually the ability to choose between a negative emotion or an emotion of love. Remember that our outer world is a mirror image of our inner self. Choosing between shoe colors is fine but since the choice is made in the physical world and not in the inner mental world, it does not bring any lasting fulfillment. Choosing between shoe colors in the physical world is actually playing around in the image of the mirror. Choices made in our thoughts such as choosing between a negative thought or a loving thought, bring lasting fulfillment and are reflected back to us in the physical realm. Making a change on our inside is the only way to lasting change and fulfillment.

When Source Energy is our guide in this world, we can use our navigation signals, called emotions to lead the way. At any given time, we have the ability to choose the freedom that lies inside the choice of alignment. To make an "aligning" choice is to first make a choice in the mind. If one is truly aligned with the light and love of the universe, the only emotion to feel will be that of Consciousness, which is love. The way you feel will be your best indicator that you are "off track" in life. Again, Source does not feel depressed or anxious. The One Consciousness is in all things. Without black, there would be no white. There is no need to compare. Within each of the disparities is Consciousness itself. Consciousness does not feel that one creation is better than another. How could it? Consciousness is the creator of all things. You and your thoughts are an individual and unique expression of Consciousness. Choosing to think divinely that the One Consciousness loves you, is to come into alignment with truth and therefore you will feel good. Feelings of anxiety or depression are emotional forms of energy designed purposefully to let you know you have lost your way. These emotions, when left unchecked and therefore completely identified with, create the needed suffering to help a person to come back into alignment and truth.

Feeling negative emotions is a healthy human aspect of life on earth. Negative emotions are like the bumpers placed in the gutters of a bowling lane to help a small child keep his/her bowling ball on course. This is all well and good. When a person feels a negative emotion about one of two choices, the choice they feel negative about could be like the bowling alley bumper helping to guide that individual, possibly away from a particular choice. The other aspect to this is that the person's negative emotion could be because they are looking at a particular choice through the eyes of the scared, egoic, false self rather than through the eyes of Source. Here is an example. If Source has blessed you with a creative talent but your thoughts do not believe it to be so, because of low self-esteem, and/or you were raised in a family that did not believe in this passion or creativity inside of you, you likely will not have a good feeling when thinking about your passion or whatever decision you are contemplating. In this case, the negative emotion is signaling to you that the *way* in which you are thinking about the choice is wrong. The choice *itself* may not be wrong. Source may be telling you that you are looking at the choice incorrectly.

When thinking about choices, alignment will give you the clarity to know if the choice is coming from love or the choice itself is not on the "path" of love. There really is no right or wrong answer. The idea is to make decisions not because it is the "right" choice, or what is an acceptable choice, vs. the so-called "wrong" choice. That is considered living in the ego. When aligned, purpose seems to change. Rather than the purpose being an accomplishment in the physical realm as the way to fulfillment, instead the practice of alignment becomes the path to fulfillment; from which the physical world becomes the reflection.

A little about right and wrong, black and white, and other opposites. Allow yourself to be free with the understanding that part of the unique aspect to this world we live in are the polar opposites. If you are searching for yourself in this world and coming up empty handed, that is a good thing. By doing so, you have acknowledged one side to the two sides of worldly ways. All worldly things have two sides. When living solely in the world, one feels every polar opposite as if its energy is somehow their own. The loss or the win is deeply felt and personal. When aligned, one recognizes the polar opposites in the world, but their inner core is not attached to the wins and losses of life.

Being able to recognize that nothing in this world is permanently satisfying and/or if you are feeling a bit lost, then you are on the right track. To the ego, the notion of feeling a bit lost can be depressing. Some will go about life trying to pretend they are happy when they are not. That is fine too. When a person digs deep enough into the notion that nothing in the physical world brings long term satisfaction, they are free to choose to live from another dimension. The choice becomes clear when aligned. Living in a mental state that consists of freedom from the ego takes precedence over any worldly circumstance.

Eventually a person in the grips of deep suffering, after having tried many methods to be happy, will recognize that the so-called pleasures of the physical world are not fulfilling, nor does any negative event have influence on the stability of their alignment with the One Consciousness. You might look at others with smiling faces and wonder why it is that everyone else is happy except for you. Contrary to popular belief, this sense of uneasiness, uncertainty, or whatever you might call it, is a wonderful place to be - mentally. After all, we know emotions such as these are just like bowling alley bumpers designed to keep a person on course. Negative emotions and positive emotions, for that matter, are our guiding mechanisms. After exploring many worldly ways and not finding the missing piece to your soul, there is just one thing left to explore, and that is you. After exploring your mind and noticing that your surroundings cannot bring lasting peace, you realize that you have been looking in the wrong places.

There are a couple of hurdles to overcome when you realize fulfillment is obtained within. The first is losing the habitual mind pattern of continuing to "seek" anything. Another hurdle is accepting that the mind cannot be trusted when left alone. Only through alignment comes wisdom and fulfillment. It is a tough gig at first to give up the habitual addiction to stuff, but not for the reasons you might think. Even after peace floods the mind with love, the years of conditioning that created a habit to "seek" elsewhere for fulfillment must be acknowledged. As always, the onus is on the individual to perform the mental work of alignment. After alignment, the only work remaining is to reprogram the mind to healthy patterns until the positive flow of love energy whisks you away. After that, it is all love and peace.

Alignment is the last option a depressed person wants to take. The world and its contents are empty, but because of a deep attachment to the physical world, a person will find it extremely difficult to look within. That was the case for me. I can say that I am grateful for the suffering I experienced because it forced me to look elsewhere for happiness. At some point, you must look within and to your amazement, the entire universe's abundant vibrations are found. The key is that each individual needs to do it for him/herself. No one is handed lasting fulfillment in the form of worldly possessions, a pill, or even a self-help book. Lasting fulfillment is only felt when you search, ask, and receive. If you are waiting for a "god" figure far away in a mysterious place called Heaven to hand you abundance while your vibration consists of lack, you will be waiting a very long time. The depression that resides within you emits a very different vibration.

When aligned to Consciousness, you know who you truly are through your own unique vibrational version of Consciousness. This is where you will find lasting fulfillment. This is also where you will find a vibration that when emitted, the universe will echo back to you the love you have always wanted.

Learning how to align is a choice. Learning how to drop negative emotions such as anxiety is also a choice. Most of what an individual experiences on a day-to-day basis are learned habitual patterns built on past conditions. Once alignment is attained and negativity is seen more like a friendly helper to guide our way, it is up to the individual to make the choice of freedom each and every second of every day. This is not a one-size-fits-all program, nor is freedom and fulfillment a one-time choice. You will have to choose alignment constantly as the physical world presents itself in many different ways of expression. Remember, just as you are, so is the world an expression of the One Consciousness. It, too, is doing exactly what you are doing. It is also evolving. It is a friendly place when seen from the vantage point of coexistence. "Friendly" just means unconditional love. Allow life, the people in it, and everything physical to be that which it desires to be at any given moment. There is no right or wrong. In return, you will receive the same "permissions." That is, to live, make "mistakes" (even though there are none), enjoy peace, and allow everyone else to do the same. Through this mindset, full abundance will be yours - abundance, being attained through alignment, not the ego.

Children who grow up with parents that were not aligned with Source (i.e., aligned with their ego instead) will take on that same way of living. One child may adapt more easily to the egoic patterns of living than the other, making them appear much more "functional" than the other child. One child may not adapt to the egoic way of living because the learned egoic patterns do not resonate with their deeper self. The one Universal Consciousness that connects us all may desire more "awareness" through one person than another. A child of parents that were aligned with the ego may suffer greatly because their deeper self is in direct contrast to the egoic nature learned as a child. Their inner essence of "who" they are will not resonate with "who" their parents told them they are. If living from the ego, a child will feel it necessary to explain this to his/her parents and have them understand. When aligned, others are accepted as they are, and one feels no need to "convince" anyone of anything.

The contrasting difference on the inside of a person having been raised by egoic parents causes a confusion about love. Their inner essence knows truth but to accept this truth would put them in direct opposition to their parents - or so it would seem to a young child. Disagreeing with parents, obviously does not mean that the child dislikes his/her parents, but in the child's mind, it is felt this way. The child senses and knows the parents' deep love for them and yet the child also sees through the false self of the parents. To the child, the parents' "truth" of One Consciousness should be obvious to them. The child cannot imagine that the parents do not know the peace that passes all understanding. In the child's mind, everyone must know the true connection to Source Energy just as he/she does. A child will assume his/her parents also know this truth. The child assumes the parents are acting with purpose, in complete disregard of, and in opposition to, One Consciousness.

What is obvious to the child, may not be obvious to the egoic parent. The child may act in complete disregard for his/her own alignment to Source in an effort to please/love their parents. To the child, to act in accordance with his/her own alignment is to "not love" their parents. This is the basis for suffering. A child's disregard for his/her own alignment causes suffering. Suffering is also present in him/her because he/she simply cannot believe that his/her parents do not know what he/she knows. The child's knowledge is not factual, academic, or worldly knowledge. Instead, the child's knowledge is about what he/she thinks truth of Consciousness is itself, that love is everywhere. The child sees no reason for the fearful mindset of the parents. He/she watches the parents live from the egoic place of fear. The child may feel as if disagreeing with the parents is to not love them. Most likely the child does not understand the way he/she feels or even knows what to call it. The child may feel suffering when he/she tends to his/her own alignment because he/she has been raised to think that acting in accordance with his/her own alignment will result in harm or at the very least, upset their parents. Of course, the child would not know to call what he/she is feeling as alignment and the child will not be fully aligned. Rather, the child is just closer to alignment in that there are less layers of the false self to remove due to having spent less time in the world. A five-year-old child has not had as much time as a thirty-year-old to learn these false patterns. Children are also born with the false self in them. The child may suffer because this type of living does not resonate with him/her.

The parents, living from the ego, want what is best for the child out of love. Unfortunately, the parents, living from the ego, do not know love to be the same as the child living closer to alignment knows it to be. Both the parent and the child are ignorant in that they are unaware that the other cannot see love from their vantage point. They both feel as if the other is acting in complete disregard to "love" and desperately wants to be understood. There is an opportunity to make a choice, but either choice appears to bring suffering to the child.

However, once true alignment is made, the confusion is cleared up.

From the child's perspective, the false self of the parent is seen for what it truly is. The child is able to recognize that he/she does not have to choose between love of the deeper self or love of the parents. The child can now see the parents as living from a place of confusion and acting according to their own truth. The love expressed from the parents, while egoic and empty, was truly their best version of love as they knew it. When the child is truly aligned, he/she recognizes this. This is the wisdom that sets the child free to feel the peace that passes all understanding. Of course, the parents could align before the child does and come to the same points of wisdom I just expressed.

When aligned, the child recognizes not just that his/her parents loved him/her from the only vantage point they knew at that time, but also that the view from which the child saw the relationship was based on the false self. The child may have felt his/her own opinion/version of himself/herself when expressed, was a form of "not loving" his/her parents. This erroneous thought is replaced with truth when aligned. In this way, the child has the freewill to choose to think differently about a situation. This is an enormous freedom. The egoic self may think the only choice is to change the situation to find peace. Obviously, changing a situation is in the physical and material world. We know that the material world is a mirror reflection and to make changes there is like running a brush down the proverbial mirror instead of running the brush through our hair. Again, lasting change needs to be made in the mind first. Changing situations can be a good thing, but for mental peace, this decision should be secondary.

Having the choice to be able to think differently about situations is liberating. If our thoughts are incorrect about enormously important things such as the way we feel and process information, then we can choose to process our entire world differently. To do so, is to change the world. Looking into the mirror's reflection, also known as the world around you and choosing to see it as the One Consciousness sees it is liberating. This will resonate deeply when aligned. Seeing the world around you as Source sees it, will change it. This is also supported by the quantum physics Observer Theory. Simply observing something can change its behavior. Imagine your power to change things not just by observing, but by thinking differently about what you are observing and then make a change.

The idea is not to control the universe. That would be an egoic thought from the false self and very limiting. Better, is to align ourselves to the One Consciousness. Consciousness is smarter than we are - it created us. It is through alignment with Source that we can drop the illusion of our disconnection to Source, through which all things are created. In this dimension, our situations, thoughts, and presence become divine. A huge veil is removed. A burden is lifted. We become the light. Darkness ceases to exist. Dichotomies disappear and love is all there is.

True peace does not start with anything in the material world. Shortly after you purchase a new car, the feeling of newness will subside and something else will be desired. Without alignment, this endless cycle to nowhere is found in all material things. It is in relationships, love, finances, religion, and so on. Choosing alignment first will bring lasting peace. After alignment, love, relationships, finances, and religion are all wonderful additions to life. You are fulfilled prior to receiving those material things and it is in that state of mind that they are enjoyed to their fullest. When aligned, the coming and going of material objects are welcomed. Life is not a struggle. This happens when we choose to align our thoughts to Source. In this way, our egoic thoughts, based on conditioning from the past, are replaced with infinite thoughts of wisdom.

Some people subconsciously act in opposition to who they really are. You may have developed a role as a child to behave in a certain way because you knew this behavior would keep your parents happy. Maybe you developed a behavior that kept you safe from anything you deemed as a threat. This habit was developed at an early age and therefore adopted to be a subconscious "truth" for living. In this way, you may have subconscious and automatic responses to situations. When the situation cannot be manipulated in the same way you maneuvered situations in your younger years, you feel out of control. This manipulation refers to the illusion of influencing your parents in a codependent relationship. When parents send loving signals to you only when you behave in a certain way, you become accustomed to "manipulating" the situation by changing your behavior to control your parents' responses and love.

As you grow up, anxiety may persist when the subconscious, dysfunctional, and illusory ways do not work in the world. You may try to attain love in this way. Suffering occurs when you are aware that it is wrong but do nothing to change your thoughts about it. To amend thoughts would mean that your entire belief system is faulty, so you choose to suffer rather than experience the "unknown." This unknown has been shared by the egoic parents as being a horrible place. Denial of yourself occurs when you choose to live according to the behavior of others. This people-pleaser mentality does not allow you to express yourself as your own unique expression of Source. This denial of self was created at a young age for protection and serves as an act of violence against yourself in your adult years.

Your behavior changes with every person you encounter in an attempt to create stable emotions you lacked as a child. This places your own source of happiness onto another human being. Your happiness now depends on how well you are able to create a desired response in another person. The pattern mostly goes unnoticed as you move through life suffering, as if the world does not love you, because you are unable to recreate what you have learned as a child. Unknowingly, your motive for living has nothing to do with your own desires found in true alignment. In fact, you do not even know what your desires are. All you know is that the world is not reciprocating in the way you once found truth as a child. This subconscious belief and survival system is extended into every relationship - spouse, teacher, friend, business, etcetera - all are met with an illusionary form of how life works. In some cases, you will behave completely differently around different people, saying contradictory statements and not even be able to see this for yourself.

Chapter Twenty-Nine

BELIEF

Recognizing that what we hold near and dear to our heart as "truth" could actually be hurting us, is crucial to grasp. Even more importantly, being able to know truth in a way that was never revealed to us, is very significant. By choosing alignment we are able to see how profound this choice is. The reason this choice is so remarkable is because the very thing that creates the suffering actually frees us from it. That thing is belief.

Very few people ever challenge their beliefs. They hold fast to a thought and through doing so, they make it their reality. Again, perception is reality, right? Belief that your own creation has been formed on purpose by a supernatural power is liberating. To truly understand that at this very moment, doing exactly what you are doing, while thinking the exact thoughts you are currently processing are all perfectly in line with Source Energy, is freeing. You, your actions, and thoughts, right now at this exact moment in time, are all the divine expression of the One Consciousness. You, your thoughts, actions, and beliefs, have been filtered through life (e.g., via parents, hardships, etcetera) in a divine way to create the masterpiece Source calls "you." Knowing that you were created with purpose, passion, love, and peace, is wonderful. When you recognize that absolutely everything about you was created for the fulfillment of the One Consciousness, you become free. This includes everything and excludes nothing. Your thoughts, desires, and deeds have all been anointed by Source Energy.

You must realize that to believe in your human limitations is just as much a truth as to believe in your divinity with the infinite Universal Consciousness. Whatever you choose to place your faith into, is your divine right. Belief separates us - not color, status, finances, or anything else. Belief is more than what you can physically see with your eyes. It is through alignment that all things are unconditionally seen as divine, and the world becomes a place of peace and love. When aligned, belief in something greater than your physical self is sensed and known. Once a new belief is attained through alignment, truth is seen, but the removal of habitual patterns, and layers of the false self are shed one layer at a time.

Because of the false self, our interpretations of events are usually incorrect. When aligned, we do not use our false self to navigate the world. Those ways are tainted with misconceptions that were formed through interpretations perpetuated while looking into the mirror image. Nothing in that mirror image is sustainable. Acting on interpretations of the world in that sense creates more of the same devastation and suffering. It is only through alignment that wisdom is gained. Wisdom provides a clear mental picture from which to create in the material world. It is the belief in alignment that allows for the peace that passes all understanding. Belief is not something handed to a person. Searching the world for a pill, meditation, religion, or anything else to "give" you what you are looking for is fine as long as you have the wherewithal to tweak the modality to your own individual expression of Consciousness. You must believe that whatever it is you are searching for is already yours. Again, whatever it is you are searching for is not given first and believed in second.

As an example, notice that the false self puts the new shirt on, looks into the mirror, smiles, and feels good as you believe the shirt gave you something. In this example, you believed that the shirt would bring you a sense of joy and it was the shirt that gave you fulfillment. When in alignment, you believe you already have everything, are not lacking in anything, and when you put a new shirt on, it brings you a sense of joy but is not "needed" to feel complete. The truth is that the belief that the shirt brings us fulfillment is incorrect. The other truth is that the belief system attained by the false self is incorrect. We falsely believe we are lacking in something and search for it in the physical world.

We have the ability to believe in opposition to negative emotions without suppressing or rejecting them. When aligned, we know who we really are. When an emotion arises from a thought, one can choose to align the thoughts with that of Source. At times, thoughts can make us feel diminished, as if we are less than someone else. The act of comparing is part of the problem but believing that you are less than is the other part. When we feel diminished, we are choosing to align with the world rather than Source. The connection to Source has been lost and that is why we feel negative emotions. When feeling any negative emotion, it is best to stop and align with Source to be reminded of who you really are. In this way, you are never left alone to figure things out.

Imagine a horizontal line as being the place a person connects to Source. Below this line are negative emotions. Feeling unworthy would place you below the horizontal line of alignment. Many people feel like depression is an entity that they have no control over. We actually have control over our thoughts. The emotions that arise are less likely in our control. When depressed, you are thinking thoughts that lead you to feel depressed. The problem is not the depression or the thoughts. The problem is that you "believe" in the negative self-talk. You believe in the negative thoughts. I certainly used to believe in those thoughts. Suicidal depression stemmed from the thoughts I created while I was a kid being bullied. I also created negative thoughts because I was not academically gifted - not in the slightest. School was not only something I was not good at, but it was also not a place where I felt safe. I created all sorts of negative thoughts about myself because of these factors and more.

I am not going to try to convince you that anxiety, depression, and other negative emotions are self-generated. Take a look for yourself when aligned. Source Energy is on this imaginary horizontal baseline of love. On this line, you were created with the intention of placing you into the exact life you have now. Every moment was, and is, divine. Every milestone is divine. For me, my marriage, divorce, good and bad times with my children, my physical abilities, and the eventual loss of those physical abilities was, and is, all a part of my divine experience. The heartache, mistakes, wins, and losses are all pieces of the divine experience that shaped and molded me.

My circumstances do not dictate "who" I am. The circumstances of my life mold me into exactly the right emanation of the One Consciousness.

It is really important to understand that every time a person feels left out, or less than, shorted, hurt, they got a raw deal in life, they have a crappy brain, they have a crappy body with a crappy immune system, they said all the wrong things, that they screwed up tons of times, that they were screwed by life, and so on, the person is choosing to believe these thoughts. Some of these statements may appear true *factually* but none of it was a mistake and none of it can take away your divinity. You are on that imaginary baseline I spoke about earlier. On that line you are divine. When you feel depressed, you are choosing a thought that is below the line and not in alignment with the One Consciousness. In essence, you choose to separate yourself from Source. Source is in love with you and the rest of its creation. Nothing is outside the imaginary horizontal line of divinity except for your thoughts and that, too, is a divine way to bring on suffering to help you to return to the place of love and peace.

Above this imaginary, horizontal baseline of divine love is the inflated person. The person who thinks they are better than everyone. Not much needs to be said here except that it is also generated by thoughts that are not in alignment with Source on the horizontal baseline. Thoughts that take us below this line, such as depression, are just as much out of line with Source as thoughts that are above the baseline. A person has become wrapped up in the material world when their thoughts take them below or above that imaginary baseline of divinity. Thoughts that drop a person below, or raise them above, the baseline means that they believe more in what the material world defines them as, predicated on their own delusion. A person valuing themselves according to comparisons with the world would be just as delusional as the rose bush with a broken thorn and a few wilted petals deciding that it is a horrible bush with a horrible life when looking at a field of sunflowers. Even if the rose bush had a million moments of sunlight and warm summer rains, even if it had a human mind, it may very well focus on just the depressing aspects.

Every second of every day, we can make the conscious choice to align our unique expression of Source as it has been divinely shaped by the influences of the world, with the One Consciousness. We have the freewill to choose to be on the imaginary horizontal divine line I spoke about earlier, or not. The horizontal line is imaginary, but that mental place of divinity is not. We can think the way Source Energy thinks or we can place all of our value into a comparison's bucket and live a delusional life based on limited human thought. That is our freewill and choice.

When we choose to believe in our divinity, we have aligned with Source. At that moment, you create Heaven on earth. Heaven on earth will not last forever unless you choose to align yourself at every second of every day until the habitual patterns of the false self are replaced with the habitual patterns of your divine self. The problem is that people want Heaven on earth given to them in the same way a shirt is given to a person in the material world. Once a shirt is received, it is always yours. Heaven on earth is a little different because our minds think this place of nirvana is somewhere outside of us and needs to be searched for to be attained. Some even think they need to pay a price to get there, like cleaning up their life or praying for acceptance.

Heaven on earth is already in you. You were completely aligned with it when in the womb of your mother. Over time, and through experiences, people develop layers of the false self that hide their divinity. Habits are formed and we become identified with the material world. When we shed the false self, choose to believe in our divinity, and make this a new habit, we become new creatures on earth. Heaven on earth is attainable. This takes a bit of everyday work to break the habits of the false self. It takes no work to open the portal to Heaven. There is no physical sacrifice necessary. You do not need to sacrifice anything except for your delusional idea that you are limited somehow. It is our thinking mind that separates us from a plant, animal, or a stream. The beautiful part is that we can choose to identify with the world or with the One Consciousness.

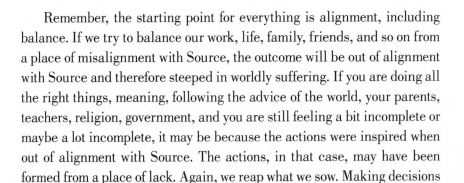

Chapter Thirty

BALANCE

Remember, the starting point for everything is alignment, including balance. If we try to balance our work, life, family, friends, and so on from a place of misalignment with Source, the outcome will be out of alignment with Source and therefore steeped in worldly suffering. If you are doing all the right things, meaning, following the advice of the world, your parents, teachers, religion, government, and you are still feeling a bit incomplete or maybe a lot incomplete, it may be because the actions were inspired when out of alignment with Source. The actions, in that case, may have been formed from a place of lack. Again, we reap what we sow. Making decisions and acting from a place of abundance is to sow and reap in alignment.

The deep vibration emitted from within the world will reflect back to you the same. Most likely there is a hidden vibration of both lack and abundance within you. There will be wonderful areas of your material world that will come very easily to you. You will just seem blessed in certain areas. These areas are different for all of us. More than likely, there is also an area inside of you that seems cursed. For example, you might always lose your keys, or cannot seem to impress your boss. Both the blessing and the curse are coming from a hidden vibration. It is a belief that was instilled at a young age that you have unknowingly adopted over the years.

These so-called good and bad beliefs that send subconscious vibrations out to the universe, supersede anything that comes out of our physical mouth when we are not in alignment to Source. No matter how hard you try, and no matter how much willpower you use, your efforts to break either the good or bad vibrations will not succeed if you are not aligned. Some people, no matter what they do, are always a success or a failure in one particular area. I have a friend that places absolutely no effort into playing pool and he continues to win games as if there is a magical force behind him. Of course, that magical force is his deep vibration and alignment to Source. We all know someone who, no matter how hard they try, seems to have the worst "luck" in a particular area. It could be anything from hitting all the red traffic lights to always forgetting to pay one particular bill. This is from a subconscious belief emitting a vibration of lack.

Balancing oneself does not mean following every piece of worldly advice. In fact, following all the worldly advice is okay as long as this advice is considered secondary to alignment. Following worldly advice alone, is a crapshoot. This is partly why we see strange dichotomies like the friend who seems to have everything, and yet takes his own life. This makes us scratch our heads and ask, why? Alignment alone does not rule out challenges or guarantee blessings. It does, however, rule out the individual from suffering through loss or lack. Alignment is balancing but it is not balancing the world's events or your physical and tangible actions. Alignment is balancing your vibration while life is springing up all around you.

It is also important to remember that even those events that cause us to scratch our heads could bloom from alignment. Neither I, nor anyone else, can tell if your actions are inspired from your own alignment. To compare and judge another is an act of the false self and does not come from alignment. Beware of that trap. Anytime we take our eyes off of ourselves is a time we have stopped being the light of the world. The only way to Heaven on earth is to align and be. All other avenues are foolish. Our relationship to others, animals, and the world will improve greatly when we give others the same divine right we give ourselves. That is, the right to be as they wish.

We have the power to bless or curse everything we do, depending on our vibration. If we do not know that we are emitting a vibration of lack, we cannot fix it. We are not guilty of any so-called wrongdoings, and we forgive ourselves. The same rights are given to others as well. We do not judge them, guilt them, or try to fix them, and we definitely forgive them, for they know not what they do. When we come to know alignment as a mental place of freedom and peace, we lose the need to judge others as a result. Our own alignment becomes too precious to trade it in for an egoic moment to condemn another. We know that this type of thought creates a vibration of discord within the body, plants a seed of lack, and will return to us in the world of physical form. This does not imply we stay positive. It means we stay aligned. That is a big difference.

Anxiety or depression can be treated much in the same way a broken arm can be repaired. We may fail to realize that anxiety is no more of a lifelong disease than a broken arm is. Healing is a choice and a belief away - continually practicing alignment until the habitual nature of the returning negative thoughts are broken. Balance is restored when we choose to believe in something other than what has not worked for so many years. There is no fight. There is no battle. There is nothing missing. Healing and Heaven are attained in aligning to Source the moment a negative energy source is detected within you. Each time you choose alignment, you have broken another link in the habitual patterns of the delusion of pain, lack, suffering, and so on. The power within you is tapped with every moment you consciously choose alignment. Alignment is a moment-by-moment practice in the physical realm that unlocks the spiritual realm.

One difference between an adult's faith and a child's faith is alignment. When a child goes out to play, he/she is, most likely, closer to being aligned. The child may be wearing a few layers of the false self. As the child explores the world, he/she does not have preconceived ideas that hold him/her back. The child runs on the front yard knowing that Source Energy will keep the lungs pumping oxygen and the heart working as it should. The child knows Source will give him/her the strength and lung capacity according to the vibration of complete alignment he/she emits. Adults can also take fearless steps forward in life knowing they are safe, sound, and in the watchful and helpful hands of Source but many do not because of conditioning and other beliefs. I make sure I am safe and sound by maintaining alignment. When/if a negative emotion arises while I am expressing a childlike faith in the form of living life to its fullest, one of two things are happening. Either my actions are not in accordance with Source, or my thoughts are not in harmony with Source. Balance is restored when I realign.

You see, life is fun, but only through alignment are life's so-called ups and downs seen as part of the fun. Through alignment, life's challenges are presented in such a way that they are seen as another moment of childlike exploration. When we are balanced in alignment we do not "want" or "need" anything to fulfill us or take away the boredom, pain, or anxiety. Some moments and achievements are ways of enhancing our fun, but they do not enhance ourselves as a person. When we are balanced, buying a new and fancy car does not complete us or add anything to who we are. Nor does the loss of a fancy car take away anything. It cannot. When you are balanced, you are already abundant, blessed, fulfilled, and secure. Nothing worldly can change that.

We enter this world as a free spirit and develop a reactionary method as a way of living. It is more clearly seen in later years. In many circumstances, people behave completely opposite of the way they were raised. For example, if as a child, you were not held as much as you needed, when you become a parent, you hold your children much more. This is an obviously harmless example of living from a place of reaction. We can live from a place of reaction due to the present situation or as I stated above from the past. There are, however, deeper subconscious patterns in which a person mostly lives from a state of reaction from the past rather than their own divine creative footprint.

Here is an example. You may have no idea that it is the presence of your overweight relative that drives you to eat healthy and exercise. There could come a time when your relative leaves and you realize that while the hard-core diet and exercise has been a great habit, it is not the source of happiness. In this instance, the happiness was gained through creating a self-image of being "better" than the relative. You may feel empty when your relative moves away because your purpose was motivated by reacting to someone else rather than through your own alignment. You may notice that all the efforts, while good, were for the wrong reason. Happiness is sometimes found in creating an identity that is as far away from what you knew as a child. Obviously, this is not true happiness, and you are searching for it while wearing a false identity.

If you look inward, you may find the underlying reason for many actions to be a habitual pattern of reactions learned during the earlier years. It is not uncommon for someone to spend their whole life trying to "prove" that they are **not** something or that they **are** something based on a reaction learned a long time ago. Suddenly an empty feeling or confusion may set in when your eyes are opened to this. Some spend their lives "pleasing" others in an attempt to give what it was they themselves were never given. This, too, is a reaction to their environment - reactionary living.

After many years of reactionary living, you may notice the path of destruction left behind. You may feel deep emptiness. You may be completely dumbfounded as to how you could have lived so many years reacting to others, rather than pursuing your divine purpose. You will have to reinvent yourself after this discovery. This emptiness can be filled with adventure as you search for what you desire. This self-discovery is a great time for alignment and balance. Through alignment, you will not learn someone else's methods of how to live life. You learn your own but, most importantly, you learn about yourself.

As I said earlier, reactionary living comes disguised in healthy ways too. You may have grown up in poverty but spent your life becoming better educated and earning a higher paying salary than your parents. This is evolution itself, whether it is seen in a negative light or a positive one. You can evolve from a place that was "squeezed" to inspire change. If change is acquired through alignment, it will be much more fruitful than if it was achieved through an unconscious decision to inflate yourself or in a reactive, subconscious way. The point I am trying to make is that no matter the action or thought, when it is borne from alignment to Source Energy, it is divine and lasting. It is more important to be aligned than anything else. Action arises out of alignment when the One Consciousness sees fit to do so. In this way, harmony precedes the discord of egoic desire.

I discovered, through alignment and balance, that I was doing and thinking mostly from reactionary means rather than "doing" through my own unique individual expression of the One Consciousness. Motorcycles became a love of mine because, at an early age, riding them stopped my habitual worry about being bullied and the academic abilities I seemed to be lacking. I still enjoy motorcycles today, but they are not needed as a reactionary measure to escape self-damning thoughts. The more layers of the false self I remove through alignment and balance, the more I see the need to inflate the ego as an illusion.

Fulfillment happens not when one receives. Fulfillment actually occurs when the layers of dysfunction, fear, and ego are removed. An incomplete human being (e.g., body ailments, relationship troubles, etcetera) with a complete and divine essence is discovered. While discovering layers of the false self, I asked myself, "Who told me I was incomplete?" No one tells us this verbatim, but humans assume this false identity as their vulnerable, infantile child form grows up. We enter the world as all-knowing Consciousness but in infant form, relying solely on another for food and love, we also exchange our deeper self for the ways of the world. Feeling the need to be the best as well as feeling less than others are both egoic ways stemming from the illusion of incompleteness. It is the influencer behind the motivating drive that determines whether a person is acting according to their own alignment or not. The activity itself is not a means to decipher if a person is acting according to their alignment to Source or not.

Sometimes parents are unable to be attentive in the present moment with their children. The child notices the lack of attention, senses fear, and assumes this form of living is acceptable. The child grows up without ever deeply knowing themselves or others. The mind has been trained to think, worry, plan, and do anything other than be highly attentive and present at any moment. This leads to the difficulty of alignment because stopping habitual thinking is considered foolish to the ego. The intense focus by the parent on everything outside of the present moment, leaves the child feeling empty. Trained to seek in the world for fulfillment, the child comes up empty handed to find love, although many will not know they are seeking love. Through the egoic means of living the life handed down to them, the child finds suffering after each short-lived and temporary worldly pleasure is gained.

Even self-destructive behaviors arise as the child feels as if they have not followed the worldly ways precisely enough to find happiness. After blaming themselves, they blame the parents or something else, not realizing there is no blame to be had by anyone. True alignment and balance sheds light on the fact that people become attached to a way of living that was inherited through fear and lack. With this knowledge, all are set free from the illusion of bondage. More importantly, it is realized that all are their own individual expression of the One Consciousness, doing their best to survive in the illusion of lack. We are all misled to believe we are incomplete. This truth is realized, and suffering is morphed into blessing. The caterpillar has changed into the butterfly, not by means of attaining wealth, love, and security in the form of material objects, but by losing the false connection to those material objects. In doing so, the inner mental world is fulfilled. The outer world will begin to reflect that, but only as a result of alignment and not as a means to an end.

If the driving motivator is "wanting" something, the vibration sent to the universe is one of paucity or lack. The universe will reciprocate that vibration and the physical creations will resemble that. The universe knows your deepest motivation because you are inseparable from it. The interesting paradox is that we do not need anything to be complete and/or to send the vibration out to the universe that says we are fulfilled. We simply need to remove our belief that says we are not already complete. Standing on that foundation, we can broadcast our signal of wholeness and receive the same vibration in physical form.

Balancing your outer physical and tangible life becomes easy when you first learn to balance in alignment. The physical world appears in just the right way when the person lives from a mental state of balance. Their actions, desires, and relationships are not tainted by unseen habitual patterns of reacting to the past. They can simply learn who they are as a person and live from a grounded and balanced self on a strong foundation.

Chapter Thirty-One

I AM & I DO

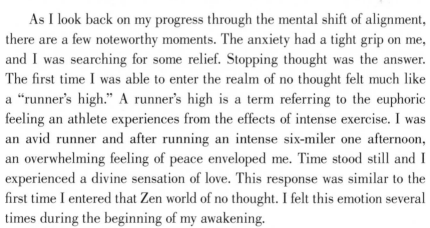

As I look back on my progress through the mental shift of alignment, there are a few noteworthy moments. The anxiety had a tight grip on me, and I was searching for some relief. Stopping thought was the answer. The first time I was able to enter the realm of no thought felt much like a "runner's high." A runner's high is a term referring to the euphoric feeling an athlete experiences from the effects of intense exercise. I was an avid runner and after running an intense six-miler one afternoon, an overwhelming feeling of peace enveloped me. Time stood still and I experienced a divine sensation of love. This response was similar to the first time I entered that Zen world of no thought. I felt this emotion several times during the beginning of my awakening.

One day, I decided to take a walk. The path I took was adjacent to a slow-moving river. It was always very beautiful, but this day was different. I suddenly felt a sensation of great peace and serenity. At the time, I was dating a woman who also experienced this feeling while meditating next to this river. It happened on separate occasions, but happened, nonetheless. I am not sure how to describe it, but when a person is aligned, it seems to be contagious to another person who is open to the vibration. Strangely, I think she was able to get into that state of consciousness because I was opening the doorway for her to see what was inside of her. You only need to feel that sense of peace just once and after that, it seems to draw you back to it time and time again.

This happened to me again while resting on a log in the woods of northern Virginia. Once more, I felt as though I had just run a 10k race, but I was completely still and quiet. A few days later, while walking through the park, I found myself overcome with the sights and sounds of life and nature around me. There were kids playing, smells of grass and trees, the view of the mountains were overwhelmingly beautiful, and the air was as pure as the earth could make it. I sat on a bench and could not believe the bliss I was feeling. Just as suddenly, I remembered where I was, and I chose to leave the realm of my "runner's high" as the concerns for life came rushing back to the forefront of my mind.

Those intense moments of peace opened a doorway to understanding that another realm existed. Those moments came with no help from drugs or alcohol. It was Heaven here on earth. I do not feel the euphoria like I did back then. It is possible that I just got used to the feeling and it all seems the same now. I do, however, feel the deep foundation of peace that resides within me. It is there wherever I go and whatever circumstance life shares with me. It is an incredible feeling still to this day and I am extremely grateful to be alive and part of life as the expression of Source Energy that I am.

Mankind is actually in search of the peace that passes all understanding. We just do not know it. The delusion is that we desire material objects thinking this will bring us happiness and they do, for a short time. Just like the addict returns to the drug that never truly satisfies, mankind continues to search for their material and worldly "fix." What mankind does not realize is that the material object, the house or new car, is empty and void, just like the inner void they are trying to fill. The enlightened one leaves the delusion of the physical form and has no desire to defend the realm he/she lives in to the people who cannot see it. The enlightened one knows it is best to just *be* the light rather than to defend or explain the light.

When you are aligned, the inner body feels good, actually it feels wonderful. When life begins to feel as if you are a part of a loving creative process, an inner transformation will take you ten times deeper into a complete sensation of satisfaction. When I feel an appreciation for life, I get goosebumps. Knowing life is unfolding around me in response to my appreciation, stirs up contentment inside me. The tide will turn as you make the energy shift from the never-ending misery of dysfunction to the infinite energy of divine wisdom. The mind and its thoughts are no longer in charge. The calling from a higher spiritual place of alignment is heard and knowing all is well takes root in your soul. Peace is accepted rather than rejected. Why would you reject peace, you ask? Because you are looking at the physical dimension of right, wrong, good, and bad. If what you see in the physical dimension is lack, you will not accept peace. You will turn it down.

There are truths and affirmations that are helpful to adopt while struggling to rid yourself of anxiety, fear, depression, or worry. Remember, most people's thinking process is based in reality. Most people think that all things are made from what can be seen and is already formed. For example, most people look at their bank account to determine their worth or at least what they can afford. Inadvertently, they place a mental parameter on where they are in life. The truth is that people box themselves into a physical dimension through a mental thought. Many people think depressive thoughts based on a real and tangible past experience. Since our thoughts are the foundation for creation, if we think according to what we physically see (e.g., our present financial situation), or if we place limits on ourselves through thinking about how bad the past was, we stay stuck.

Going forward, reprogramming your brain to take on healthy habits of self-talk will take mental work on your part. I was skeptical at first. My belief system was based in the no pain, no gain-type thinking. I was all about working very hard physically and achieving results. I am not academically blessed. I struggled in school. I entered the blue-collar world and received real results from working very hard physically. Working hard was nothing new to me. The hard part was not the work. The hard part was convincing myself that changing the things I believed wholeheartedly in as my truth, would bring lasting change. I kept at it, and I found something better than I could have ever imagined.

I am blessed by staying at peace. I deliberately think about how blessed I am. By doing so, my life unfolds in ways that help me to be and feel at peace. The more peaceful I stay, the more useful energy and love I am able to emanate. The negative energy I feel is just a loving nudge from the universe that I have lost my way. If this happens, I realign with

Source and realize the truth of peace again. There is never a moment I am supposed to feel guilty, ashamed, bad, or fearful. If these moments arise, I simply see them for what they are. They are negative energy trapped within my psyche. Each time I release this trapped, negative energy, I am not only freeing myself, but I am also freeing my children and all others I come in contact with. Directly freeing energy from others is done so through the energy field of vibration.

We have all felt the heavy atmosphere of a room full of people at a funeral. That is an example of how the invisible vibration is felt and carried by others. Conversely, we have also felt the energetic atmosphere of a great celebration such as your child's graduation or birthday. I mention these unseen vibrational energy fields to remind you that invisible vibrations of energy exist. When you are aligned, you become a higher vibration of love. Each time you choose the love vibration of alignment to Source rather than the negative energy, you are freeing your children and the people around you from this negative energy as well as yourself. You become the light of the world when you choose to align with love. This invisible vibration is the eternal life-giving energy of the One Consciousness. Each time you choose to recognize that you are not just the emanation of Source but that your spiritual roots are holy, divine, and authentically pure, you are freeing a collective of humans from the insanity of negative energy.

I will share affirmations to help guide you on your quest. You may have to veer off this path to find your own unique form of connection to the One Consciousness, but the following should get you started. I repeat these affirmations, and others, to keep me on the right path.

- At this exact moment in time, my actions and thoughts are exactly as they are supposed to be.
- I cannot get it wrong.
- Mistakes that come with feelings of guilt do not belong to me anymore.
- I am free to be me.
- My body and mind are working exactly as they should.
- Pure love, healing, and wholeness belong to me. My repayment for such great gifts is to be at peace.
- I repay Source Energy by being at peace with myself.

- I send myself love because I deserve it.
- Great things are always happening to me.
- Life is accommodating me in wonderful ways.
- Everywhere I go, I am blessed, and others are too.
- I am empowered to master my mind, body, soul, and life.

These affirmations bring us one day closer to the biggest blessing of all. When I tell myself, "At this moment, I will stay at peace," miraculously peace becomes my default emotion. Nothing can hurt me, and all is well. As long as I stay at peace, Source Energy is able to bless me more and more. The best thing about this is that this law is a compounding one. The more I stay at peace, the more peace is sent my way. Life is beautiful and wonderful. I am healthy, whole, healed, and abundant. I am loved. I am protected. There is nothing I can do that will take me off the path of fulfillment for my life. Every step I take is the right step. There is no wrong way. The more I stay at peace, the better my life's circumstances become. My only job is to stay at peace. Staying at peace is my purpose. I am so in tune with my body, I am acutely aware when I am not carrying peace in my body. When I recognize that I have picked up negative energy, I drop it without ever feeling it. All I feel is peace.

When I am hurting on the inside, I promise I will never pretend like I am not. I love every cell in my body and I know that to pretend is to hurt my body. When I am hurting on the inside, I will recognize that this is a sign to align. I will stop whatever I am doing and will send love to every cell in my body. In this way, the darkness cannot survive the light and I am immediately restored to the loving vibration of Source Energy. I recognize that there is an easier way to live by allowing energy to flow through me rather than resisting it. The body feels dense when filled with negative energy. This negative, dense energy is just an illusion and I open myself up to allow it to pass right through me. By doing so, I release any tension I have built up to "battle" the negative energy. I now know there is no battle. That, too, was an illusion. By dropping the resistance to negative energy, I allow myself to see what negative energy truly is. It is not as big, bold, scary, and strong as I thought it was. In fact, anxiety, fear, and depression have nothing to cling to when I release resistance. They simply pass right through me.

By aligning to Source Energy "I am, and I do." As a human, I have a unique life of "doing" according to the pure pleasures of my heart. As a unique expression and emanation of the One Consciousness, I am. It is through this combination of "being and doing" that I serve my purpose and live at peace. Through alignment, I see how comparisons, judgments, and labels are not serving my divine purpose. I easily recognize this as negative energy and I quickly realign. I am willing to let go of the human traits that create suffering in me like holding onto or resisting certain vibrations that do not belong to me. As I place a higher importance on alignment and release the human need for control, knowledge, right, wrong, and so on, I set myself free. I recognize this way of living is first manifested and created in the mental dimension and whatever is generated in the physical dimension is secondary.

I have a "safe zone" inside of me whenever I feel overwhelmed by negative energy. This internal place of peace is always available to me. All I need to do is to remember that it is there. I can simply take a single deep breath, take in the light of Consciousness, and negative energy leaves immediately. It cannot survive in the light. If the negative energy is still felt after taking the breath, there is no need to take another deep breath. What I am feeling is the remnants of its presence and soon that will also dissipate. The peace that passes all understanding resides inside me and I clearly know I am always safe. I need not struggle. I know that by placing my mental attention onto whatever I am feeling, rather than resisting, I have freed myself.

Trusting Source from a place of peace is your purpose. Everything else is fleeting. When aligned, you are willing to let go of what you know for the peace that comes with what you do not know. Therein lies the peace that passes all understanding. The only thing that matters is peace within, and I know where and how to find that at all times. The best imaginable life for me is manifested while I am in a mental state of rest. Why? In the same way the One Consciousness knows what is best for the tree and the birds, One Consciousness also knows what is best for me. It is through this trust and openness that the greatest manifestations arise in your life. In the same way the caterpillar must struggle and morph in the darkness of its chrysalis, you must trust that you are being molded so that you will eventually fly freely.

I recognize the reason for suffering is from the conditioning of our minds. It is not based on what we perceive as reality. Our conditioned minds know nothing of what is to come and that scares the false, egoic self. When you live according to what your higher self understands, you innately realize all is well. It is up to us to choose to believe this or not. When you do not believe, you suffer.

The purpose of prayer is not to "ask, receive, or thank." We give "thanks" to God, Source, or the One Consciousness by staying aligned. We "ask" by believing. We "receive" by becoming vibrationally aligned to what we have asked for. That is it. It is really that simple. All the work is done mentally. Make no effort on the physical realm until you have first secured the mental realm. Physical effort is nice and rewarding when it follows mental alignment. Physical effort done without alignment is futile and fleeting.

It is quite scary to the spiritual essence, peering through the eyes of the human body, to drop the pain and suffering. Years of being told by the physical world (i.e., parents, school, religion, government, and so on) that the physical is all there is, takes a while to erase. Habitual patterns and conditioning have been deeply ingrained within the human psyche. They were believed to be our absolute truth, nonetheless, they were an absolute lie. However, no one is at fault. The physical world is not to blame. Firstly, blame is another form of the false self. Blame is an egoic trap. It contains negative energy. To harbor blame inside the body is as harmful as drinking poison. Secondly, those worldly entities were living according to the only truth they knew. Even though it was not helpful to the spirit, it was in fact, their truth. If you do not tell your child not to play in the street and the child is hit by a car, would you blame the child? Of course not. People who have steered their own life, or others through their own illusion of the false self, are not at fault.

Chapter Thirty-Two

OUR PATH

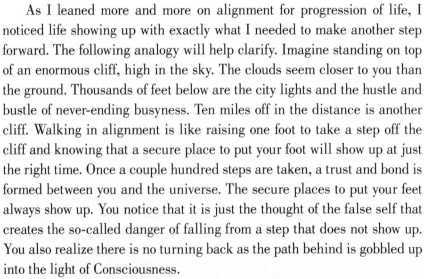

As I leaned more and more on alignment for progression of life, I noticed life showing up with exactly what I needed to make another step forward. The following analogy will help clarify. Imagine standing on top of an enormous cliff, high in the sky. The clouds seem closer to you than the ground. Thousands of feet below are the city lights and the hustle and bustle of never-ending busyness. Ten miles off in the distance is another cliff. Walking in alignment is like raising one foot to take a step off the cliff and knowing that a secure place to put your foot will show up at just the right time. Once a couple hundred steps are taken, a trust and bond is formed between you and the universe. The secure places to put your feet always show up. You notice that it is just the thought of the false self that creates the so-called danger of falling from a step that does not show up. You also realize there is no turning back as the path behind is gobbled up into the light of Consciousness.

It took quite a few years for me to eliminate the habitual patterns of suffering and lack. The peace that passes all understanding has been with me for the last several years. I became more aware, more of the time, but forty years of anxious habits formed a body memory that would take time to release. I realize some people have a miraculous awakening where suddenly they have "seen the light" and it was all bliss and harmony after that. In those instances, a habitual pattern in the body did not need to be broken. There are many forms of awakenings, like the story of a Buddha who needed to return to solitude for many years after realizing he was not at the expected point of enlightenment.

When aligned, people and material things will show up at just the right time to lend a helping hand. At just the right time, a zero percent credit card showed up in my mailbox. It is no longer a strange thing to have the helping hand of life reach out for me. It has become normal. The truck I was led to purchase a few years ago served its purpose in a way I did not see at that time. When I look back now, I can see how it manifested into my life and became a helpful asset for the many, many times I moved. Eventually, the universe would send me a sign to trade it in for a fuel-efficient vehicle. I had no idea the universe was intending to get me into this affordable car so that my daughter and I could tour the great sequoia trees of California in comfort.

To the ego, life works in mysterious ways. When seen from alignment, life happens on purpose and in harmony. Perspective is everything. There is so much more valuable information to the story about the truck. We know thoughts equal destiny and they create emotions. If I spent my emotional energy thinking about how my eighteen-year-old truck was falling apart, I would be focusing on the negative, thereby emitting a vibration that speaks to the universe as "reflect back to me negative." However, I saw the truck falling apart as an opportunity for another blessing and so my vibration was returned to me in harmony. Challenges will always come. They are either seen as obstacles or blessings. Depending on what vibration is emitted is what will be reciprocated. Not all of the time, but most of the time.

When aligned, we walk through life using our alignment to guide the way. That is to say, we see the world as it really is. A wonderful place of love and opportunity. By doing so, with every footstep into the unknown, blessing is the solid foundation created to place your foot on. This is only accomplished by releasing the ego and holding firm to Source. Releasing the ego is not quite the right words, but from an egoic point of view it may make better sense when said that way. Ultimately, the ego does not even exist when aligned. There is nothing to release or get rid of. When aligned, the ego is about as present as darkness is with all the lights turned on. Negativity is simply a sign that you are not aligned. You either are having thoughts not in alignment or an action that is not in alignment. That is it.

The figurative road ahead will always be paved according to the vibration you emit. More of whatever is on your heart will be given to you.

Practicing alignment is not the right verbiage but it might make the most sense to anyone starting out on this journey. Alignment is not really practiced, nor is it a place to get "to." Alignment is the shedding of human ignorance. Dropping the habitual nature of the ego is what needs to be practiced. I was one of those people. While I was following what appeared to me to be the right path for my life, I was suffering and causing suffering for others. With each failure, I would forge forward with more energy - to no avail. The problem was I was using egoic and false self-processes. Once I made a switch to alignment, my outer world changed.

During my transformation, I vacillated between both mindsets. I knew the old ways I lived my life were not working, but this new way of taking a step without fear, worry, and anxiety seemed impossible. I had all sorts of questions pop up. How could I trust in something I cannot see? Do I have to lose my house and car and live like a monk? Will I lose my job? What if my life unfolds in a worse way? I took baby steps. Within the two minutes of alignment, I practiced each day, I allowed myself to mentally go completely to Source. That is to say I stopped thought until my timer "woke me up." I was not really sleeping. I was alert. Actually, more alert than I have ever been, but to the ego, when I first started this practice, it appeared like I was asleep and doing nothing. I was afraid to stop thinking as if the thoughts were staying one step ahead of an ugly world from which I needed to protect myself.

Eventually, I noticed nothing horrible happened to me during these two-minute sessions of no thought. Specifically, nothing worldly or material harmed me, but mentally I noticed a big difference. I became mentally lighter after each time. It was through these short windows I would see clarity and abundance. I did not realize it at the time, but I was being pulled back into that. If I skipped a day, I would feel less balanced. I would feel "off." With each passing day of alignment, I would shed another layer of the false self and find myself in a new way.

I remember about six months ago thinking I have finally found true happiness and peace. I thought there was no way I could be happier than I was at that very moment. I was wrong. I have deepened the peace somehow. Well, maybe the peace has deepened me. Perhaps, forty years of anxiety and depression have placed millions of layers of egoic unhappiness onto me and I have just completely forgotten what it is like to be free. With the shedding of each layer comes another moment of bliss that does not seem like it can be topped, and yet it does somehow. I know tomorrow will bring another moment of joy as the challenges make a way for another blessing to occur.

I guess this is "walking by faith." None of it is done in the physical realm until it is done in the mental realm, as far as alignment is concerned. Alignment, when practiced right, is to be mentally aligned with Source before and during any and all material and worldly things. This is the key to lasting peace - align and then do. You cannot get it wrong. Not because you cannot make mistakes, but because when aligned, a "mistake" is in accordance and in harmony with Consciousness itself. Trees die. Ants get stepped on. Are those mistakes, or are the events of the world just as they should be? You will know the answer to that question when aligned. The ego thinks it knows the answer. Enjoy the evolution of life through you. It is all there is to do.

It is obvious that people enjoy the feeling that comes with good experiences. They seek experiences expecting a certain "good" feeling and stay away from others that might give them a "bad" feeling. What may not be so obvious is that the experience is not necessary to have the so-called good feeling. While living from the false self, the bucket list might contain different things than living aligned. As I sit on my back porch in alignment, my bucket list is to feel the way I feel for as long as I can before I kick the bucket, pun intended. I have no desire at this moment other than to feel the deep peace that comes with alignment. Any physical event completed on a bucket list could complement the way I feel, but it would never bring the satisfying feeling of knowing the abundance I already have.

Going through life while in alignment to Source is to have the feeling of peace and fulfillment as determining factors for the manifestations that arise. There is no more "steering the ship" called life when life is lived in this matter. We let go of control through alignment, thus we are nudged by the wisdom of Consciousness rather than the cleverness of the destructive and selfish ego. Within all of us are egos laced with fear, disguised in the rational lies of insufficiency, and drowning mankind in negative emotions such as anxiety and depression. I took a leap of faith to practice moments of no thoughts of past, future, no judgments, and with no labels when my mind and body were crushed in suffering.

I was only willing to try, what I thought was illogical, because I was mentally and physically broken. It does not take suffering to find peace for those who search for it. Someone like myself, stubborn in my own ignorance, needed to feel this agony before I looked within. As I write this, I wonder what blessing is next for me. If you are wondering what else will go wrong in your life, you are living from the false self. You may be emitting a vibration unbeknownst to you that says, "Hand me more pain." It was not so long ago that I mouthed the words I thought would bring me peace and instead received more suffering. I was bouncing from one life event to another in the hopes I would eventually catch a break. Forty years on the hamster wheel could not teach me what I learned inside the very first two minutes of the stillness of my own mind.

Two minutes at a time will not get you to Heaven on earth. Those two minutes may help to remove the barrier between you and the proverbial lottery ticket you have always had in your possession. The world will take a toll on us if we allow it through our thoughts. Imagine what your thoughts would be if you were just a few years away from death. Those thoughts would not be the same ones a person has when living in the grips of anxiety or depression. I scooped a dead bug from the pool and noticed the finality of it. That finality will be me someday. Do I really want to live the rest of my years in an illusion like the fictitious monster under the child's bed? That bug may have experienced a more well-rounded life than I did as an anxious person hanging on every egoic thought in the name of "protecting myself." Without alignment, the ego runs the body like the rag doll in the dog's mouth. We are pulled this way and that by what we think are life events, but it is really our thoughts and not the events at all.

The mind is an awesome instrument when used in conjunction with alignment. The body works harmoniously with Source. High blood pressure, unhealthy habits, headaches, etcetera are greatly reduced when the mind is returned to its source from which all life is manifested. Sleep improves and peace resides inside the body. The need for willpower to overcome personal obstacles, addictions, and fears, disappears as alignment forms the desire within the mind to simply be at peace. The short-lived and temporary energy from willpower is no longer necessary as alignment changes the desire inside a person to make the right choices. No effort is needed at all.

Chapter Thirty-Three
LOST & FOUND

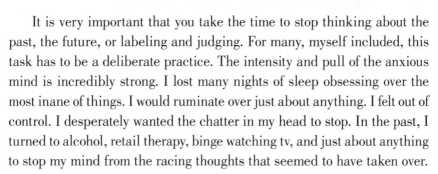

It is very important that you take the time to stop thinking about the past, the future, or labeling and judging. For many, myself included, this task has to be a deliberate practice. The intensity and pull of the anxious mind is incredibly strong. I lost many nights of sleep obsessing over the most inane of things. I would ruminate over just about anything. I felt out of control. I desperately wanted the chatter in my head to stop. In the past, I turned to alcohol, retail therapy, binge watching tv, and just about anything to stop my mind from the racing thoughts that seemed to have taken over.

Every day, I would take just a few moments to deliberately orient my mind's attention away from whatever it wanted to think about on its own. At first, I redirected my mind to positive and uplifting messages. After a while, my mind would not hear the audio. It would ignore the sounds and voices of whatever I turned on and go back to its incessant patterns.

Years ago, I spent time with a relative who was suffering from dementia. Two or three days per week we would play cards. She was not herself at all. Many moments were filled with anger and confusion. She did inconceivable acts that are too horrible to mention. Nearly every day she would have a two- or three-minute window of complete lucid thought. One day while playing cards, she looked at me as if she had not seen me in months. She said to me, "I am scared that I am going to go back there again." I asked,

"Where?" She answered, "To that place where I am so lost." We shared a few more words and just as quickly, she returned to her former delusional, angry self.

Just like that relative seemed to become conscious and aware of the truth for just two minutes at a time, I seemed to do the same. In the middle of cleaning, shopping, or even in the middle of a panic attack, I would seem to "wake up" and realize I was more or less being taken over by something that was not me. Many times, these moments of clarity would last just for a few minutes and back to the automatic and painful struggle I would go. I was unable to stop it with willpower. I could redirect my attention with something like positive audio during the day, but the nights were horrific.

Sleep is so desperately needed. Sleep is not only restorative, but reparative. It is during sleep that our body and mind can begin to repair the damage done by the day. Obviously, when the mind wants to go on its insane autopilot of habitual thinking, redirecting the mind to a movie marathon or self-help stuff does not allow for sleep. My body would shut down automatically after a few days of no sleep. Every three days or so, I would sleep for three or four hours straight. I would wake up at 2 am and notice that I was thinking about things that could be handled during daylight hours. It would be as if I was being taken over by thought while sleeping and the process of thinking too much is what woke me up. It is hard to explain but I assume many go through the same.

The time to "fix" this problem is not in the middle of the night when the mind is racing. The body is too far gone being taken over by habitual thought patterns. Just like my relative with dementia, there is no controlling it at that point. The way to get yourself some well needed sleep is by practicing "controlling" the mind when the body/mind is not influenced by the habitual negative energy patterns. Find moments when you are calm throughout the day. These are the times to practice no thought.

Of course, no thought refers to no judgments, labels, or thinking about the past or future. No thought is obtained naturally by some people. Some can simply look at the sky and feel good without using descriptive words to describe what they see. They can look at the sky and enjoy it without "thinking." I am able to do that now. I was incapable of doing that before alignment. In the past, I would look at the sky, but my mind would immediately think about the past, the future, or anything other than feeling good in that silent and still moment.

As a matter of fact, I am now able to keep a calm mind during more stressful events. However, you must practice "controlling" the mind during the "easy" times first. Over time, you will be able to do this during more difficult periods. I am now able to fall asleep and stay asleep all night. During stressful times, I now am able to notice the tension in my body and mind without it consuming me. I am able to say to myself, "I am feeling anxious." As I notice the anxiety, I can separate myself from it and its intensity decreases, eventually going away all together.

A person struggling with overeating must choose to eat healthy and exercise in order to sustain weight loss. In the same way, a lifelong change must be made to eliminate anxiety. There is no "one and done" method. During the good times, one will need to practice no thought so they have the skills to do this in the middle of the night when their mind is racing. By placing the mind's attention on the sensations received from all five senses, you can take control of the mind. Practice sensing without critiquing. No labels, judgments, etcetera. Just notice how the five senses are relaying information to the brain. The air feels cold, or the smell is strong.

Do not dramatize the senses. Practice noticing those senses and then welcoming them as a sensual perception, not as a problem. You are training the mind that "you" have control. I did not want to do this in the beginning. I wanted relief but I did not want "me" to be the relief "giver." It kind of sucks to find out that I was the source of all my problems, *and* I was the answer. Since I have the key to my own happiness, what does that say about the past fifty years of my life?

I felt like that meant that I was shooting myself in the foot and blaming others, all the while holding the smoking gun in my hand. I thought, "How can I hold the key to my happiness?" That would mean I would feel pretty guilty and shameful. I thought, "If I do not really have a problem, then who is to blame - me?" This brought on more feelings of guilt and shame. I felt like I lost so many good years of my life and hurt so many others.

The truth is, when we are operating as the false self, we are only able to see from that vantage point. Holding ourselves accountable for our behavior, while under the influence of the egoic self, would be like holding a small child accountable for sticking their finger into an electrical socket.

What you do not know, you do not know. To beat yourself up about it, is to return to the ways of the false self. Loving ourselves within the alignment to Source Energy leaves no room for negative energy. All is love when aligned.

This also means that in order to "save face" as the egoic entity, you have to consistently believe in the lies of your egoic ways. Whether you are pretending not to know the truth in order to save face or you truly do not understand the truth, does not matter. What you perceive about another person's journey is insignificant in your own alignment. Our own personal alignment is more important than anything else. Judging, labeling, and so forth have no place in alignment. The negative energy of the false self desperately wants to stay alive within you. It will create myriad ways to take you out of your emotional state of peace.

From time to time, you may need to remind yourself to keep the focus on you. There is an addiction to the negative energy of the ego. At times, the mind and body will feel good about things that only strengthen the ego. You may feel good when the confrontational neighbor is beaten up by a burglar, or the person that was tailgating you on the highway is pulled over by the police. The negative energy built up from the feeling of ill treatment could have been released at the moment the energy was felt. In those examples, the ego holds onto negative energy and waits to disperse it later.

Accumulating negative energy in this way leads to problems. It may not present a problem in small doses and for short time periods, however, if left alone inside the body, negative energy progressively gets worse. It presents as any number of ailments such as anxiety, insomnia, depression, heart disease, back pain, and gut issues. When we align ourselves, we free the mind and body from all energy that does not serve us. We become one with the energy source that created us, and the peace that passes all understanding takes up residence in our mind. With practice, in just two minutes a day, you can make the switch to a healthier life.

It all begins and ends with you and your mind. There is nothing in the world that will bring you happiness, and conversely, there is nothing that can bring you unhappiness. To believe otherwise, is to place all your poker chips on a losing bet. Fear not, because the One Consciousness loves you unconditionally and will welcome you into its loving arms when your time on earth is up. There is no need for worry or guilt. If you do, you might just be lost.

Chapter Thirty-Four
BEING THE LIGHT AS AN EMPATH

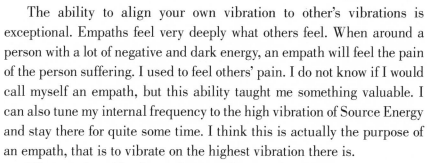

The ability to align your own vibration to other's vibrations is exceptional. Empaths feel very deeply what others feel. When around a person with a lot of negative and dark energy, an empath will feel the pain of the person suffering. I used to feel others' pain. I do not know if I would call myself an empath, but this ability taught me something valuable. I can also tune my internal frequency to the high vibration of Source Energy and stay there for quite some time. I think this is actually the purpose of an empath, that is to vibrate on the highest vibration there is.

What good would it do to vibrate on the same low frequency of someone who is suffering? Two people in a negative vibrational state increase the amount of negative energy in the world. When an empath stays on the higher vibration, they are contributing to healing. Crawling into the ditches of despair with someone who is deeply suffering does nothing to help him/her, you, or the world. Negative energy increases discord in the body. There is no good reason to create discord in your own body and I certainly do not think that brings healing to others. It just doubles the misery. An empath can be the light and be empathetic and compassionate, all the while staying on a higher vibration of healing and wholeness. In this way, the light removes the darkness. I believe empaths are called to align with

Source while in the company of the "lost" so the light of the world shines brighter and brighter.

It is through this healing light of the empath that true compassion and empathy can become the biggest help to those suffering from despair. Keeping the light bright and helping others is the way. The bar should be set higher for those in pain. Even those suffering can join us on the high-flying vibration of love and peace while we show them compassion and care. Assuming someone is incapable of crawling out of their own hole would be a huge disservice to that person. Instead, we should shine our light brighter so he/she can see the way to join us in peace.

Chapter Thirty-Five

RECOGNIZING THE EGO

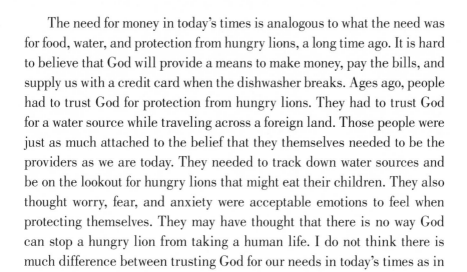

The need for money in today's times is analogous to what the need was for food, water, and protection from hungry lions, a long time ago. It is hard to believe that God will provide a means to make money, pay the bills, and supply us with a credit card when the dishwasher breaks. Ages ago, people had to trust God for protection from hungry lions. They had to trust God for a water source while traveling across a foreign land. Those people were just as much attached to the belief that they themselves needed to be the providers as we are today. They needed to track down water sources and be on the lookout for hungry lions that might eat their children. They also thought worry, fear, and anxiety were acceptable emotions to feel when protecting themselves. They may have thought that there is no way God can stop a hungry lion from taking a human life. I do not think there is much difference between trusting God for our needs in today's times as in yesteryear. People worried just as much then as today.

We do not consciously choose to feel the emotion of worry while trying to get the bills paid. Worry and struggle have taken the place of trust in God, Source, or The One Consciousness. Negative emotions and the habitual pattern of believing that they need to exist in our lives, is deeply ingrained in us. We do not even know we are putting all our trust in something that will not free us. The very thing we are trying to free ourselves from (i.e., anxiety and worry) is the thing we are using to release ourselves from. We mistakenly think that to worry about our children or finances is to "care" about them.

Have you ever said, "I do not care anymore. I give up. I am tired of this world, and I just do not care anymore." What we do not realize is that what we really do not "care" for anymore are the emotions of worry and anxiety. We falsely think we have to give up worldly things and our sense of values when we stop caring. We falsely think the only way to stop fear, worry, and anxiety is to stop caring. We can stop worry, fear, and anxiety while continuing to care deeply.

We wrongly think we must display some level of anger if another person veered off the road and wrecked into our son or daughter's parked car. Some equate not being upset with not caring. Some feel that in order to let your child know you care; you must elevate your emotions and voice your disapproval. This only teaches the child the same.

Subconsciously, many people travel through life with this point of view. They feel it is essential to experience negative emotions while navigating life, and not doing so is equivalent to not caring. If you spill coffee on your shirt before work, it is entirely possible to mentally record that you made a mistake, change the shirt, and go to work without ever creating negative energy inside your body.

Not only is it possible to stay at peace when life's challenges happen, but it is the best way. We fear what others might think and put on a display of negative energy to show others we "care." This is a subconscious process that many do not know they are even doing. To stay at peace during difficult events sends a higher vibration of peace throughout the world, thus creating more peaceful scenarios in the physical world. More peaceful vibrations equal more worldly peace. Elevating negative emotions for any reason increases the overall negative energy in the world.

A balloon full of helium will always rise. We are like the balloon. Would placing water into the balloon help it to rise in any way? Of course not. We also know that placing negative energy into our bodies is not good for us, others, or the planet, and yet we still do it. Why? Because of a false self that is hidden so deeply within you that you do not even question its authority. It is the ego. We trust in this thing called the ego so much so, we create discord within our bodies, spread it to others, and harm our planet, all the while claiming the right to be negative.

We say things like, "They were mean to me, so I will stick up for myself and be mean right back to them." Have you ever said, "That person hurt my child, so I will give them a hard time." Some people are under the delusion of the ego, so much so, they act in total disregard for themselves and have no idea they are even doing it. I used to place an enormous amount of importance on making money as a blue-collar worker and pushing the limits of my body so far that my body physically stopped working because of injuries and sleep deprivation.

I thought it was perfectly okay to struggle, strain, and push the body to its limits. I actually was proud that I was an achiever. What I did not realize is when we neglect the human body, we create negative energy. We are acting outside of the path of natural and divine harmony. I carried around a big ball of suppressed emotions, mental pain from disidentifying with the God who created me, and physical pain. Ignoring the creator and its creation (i.e., the mind and body) brings suffering. I did this because a small, egoic entity in me said that I was not good enough to achieve financial security in this world as the person God created me to be. I did not believe that just the right amount of money would flow to me at just the right time. I thought I had to struggle and strain to obtain financial security.

This false self hides the real you from you. It is making decisions for you, and you are the star of this dysfunctional show. Others see the mess you are creating for yourself, but you cannot see that you are doing it. You are highly aware of how others are making bad choices for their lives just as they can see the bad choices you make. Others cannot see their own mistakes. They think they can, just as you think you can, but that is the delusion.

It is easy to see this entire process of disharmony in others. Look around and notice how those people that make the same dysfunctional mess in their lives continue to do it. They always have a strong emotional reason for where they are in life and why. Their emotionally charged reasons are enough to tell others to stay out of their dysfunctional mess. It is as if they want to be stuck in the quagmire. Of course, they do not know that the false self is rising up through the discord of their elevated emotions. They do not know they are defending dysfunction. They believe in what they think is the truth, but it is really the scared little ego inside them, and they think the only way forward is through the process they have always believed in. Even after years have passed and they still feel the heavy emotional weight of negative energy, they make those same decisions.

The person in the story you just read about could not possibly be you, right? Think again. There is a good chance that the divine you that is peering through those beautiful human eyes God gave you, has detached from the One Consciousness and attached its hope and faith on a scared, egoic entity. This egoic ball of negative energy is dripping wet in fear and has you believing that it is the answer to the salvation your soul desperately searches for. If you are a go-getter like me and you have the physical courage to jump from airplanes, rock climb and rappel down the face of a dam into rushing water, and soar through the air on motocross, then maybe you have the courage to trust in Source?

Something behind the scenes is running your life. Something behind the scenes is whispering to you to take that job, call out sick, push harder, take a vacation, get married, get divorced, move to Maine, use your time wisely, and always be productive. Don't you want to ensure the voice that whispers to you, that you place all of your trust in, is actually your ally? Are you still suffering from negative energy in the form of anxiety, depression, fear, worry, anger, and disharmony within? Have you tried something new, strange, and bizarre, like stopping the mind's habitual chatter for two minutes?

What voice tells you that stopping thoughts will not work? Is there something inside you that does not want you to stop all thoughts? If you are still feeling a bit uneasy about your path in life and you have not figured it out by now, what is stopping you from trying something different? Are you able to sense the ego's attempt to place roadblocks in an effort to stop this process? Why do you think that is? Could there possibly be freedom in no thought? Would the voice that keeps you on the emotional and tiresome treadmill of life go away, if you stopped thoughts for just two minutes?

Your ego is running your life and you do not know it. Stopping thoughts means shutting down the ego - the very thing you placed all your trust in.

If any of this resonates with you in just the slightest bit, you have opened the window to the light of truth. From here on out, the only thing needed is simple awareness and practice of no thought. I do not know how long it will take to rid yourself of the habitual patterns that return control back to the ego. I do know that the peace that passes all understanding is available the moment you become aware of everything I have covered here. At that moment of awareness, you have become the light and you have the choice to return to the light at every moment.

Chapter Thirty-Six

MY PEP TALK TO YOU

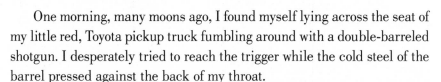

One morning, many moons ago, I found myself lying across the seat of my little red, Toyota pickup truck fumbling around with a double-barreled shotgun. I desperately tried to reach the trigger while the cold steel of the barrel pressed against the back of my throat.

I wish I could unscrew my head today and compare the scenes replayed from years ago to the way I see the world today. To all of you stuck in this mire, I have a few things to say. The first is, hallelujah, I am free! The second is, do not give up. I was right there in the trenches with you. I was there for nearly forty years. I know what it feels like to carry the heavy burden of anxiety, depression, and panic attacks.

Stay vigilant, my friends. If this old boy from Pennsylvania can do it, so can you. Once you recognize the core belief system that you use to navigate this world is faulty, you will be able to move forward. The first hurdle is coming to terms with the fact that the problem *and* the solution resides within. Conditions, paradigms, and defense mechanisms collected as a youngster to "help" you along are likely the culprit.

Yes, I understand. You were beat up, mistreated, left out in the cold, abused, and so on. Life can be hard, or perhaps you did not suffer through hardships and yet you are still depressed or anxious. The guilt you feel because you think that you do not have a reason to be depressed or anxious can also be extremely debilitating. None of that matters though. Interestingly, that is not where the problem lies. The problem is not in the tangible details of your situation. The problem is in the processing. How you process that information will determine the fate of your mental health going forward.

Sounds really ridiculous, I know. Do not do what I did and hold fast to flawed thought processing. While it is true that your pain is real, horrific, and very, very heavy, it is also true that there is a light at the end of the tunnel. Stay watchful. Get mad if you need to. Just make sure you direct all of that energy to the ego hiding inside *you*. Do not direct your energy anywhere else, nor should you direct your energy toward your own feelings of guilt.

My job was very stressful. I thought I did not like being a site manager. The cause of most of my stress was that I did not like to leave things unfinished. As a child, I operated best when I had all my tasks complete. My sister had a dog that was unable to stop chasing after a tennis ball. The dog would come back exhausted, but always chased the ball. Eventually, my sister threw two balls. The dog understood, deep inside its psyche, he must retrieve the ball no matter how tired he felt. Eventually, the dog came back with both balls in its mouth, panting and heart racing, and sat down holding both balls so she could not throw them again.

I realized I was like the dog. I would lose sleep if tasks at my job were not completed. Anyone who has run a business knows, there will always be something left undone. This drove me crazy. It was not until I changed the way I processed the information, that I found relief. It was not until I found the hidden filter in my brain and changed the way I thought that I found freedom in the middle of that stressful situation.

My job comes easy to me. Turns out, I am really good at it. I can knock off more items from the to-do list than most others. What I hated was the egoic entity inside me that made me feel bad for not having fully completed the list. Once I changed the way I mentally processed my emotions on the inside, the outside world became accommodating.

Complete alignment appears selfish from the perspective of the ego. I say the words, "I will feel good regardless of the people or situation surrounding me." From the perspective of the ego, a person should not have that much permission to feel good. It is antithesis to what we all have been taught growing up. However, from the perspective of the higher self, alignment already includes treating others well. This is true alignment.

The who, of who is at fault, is inconsequential. Trap, trap, trap. That is all I can say about that.

You hold the key to your destiny. When you continue to focus on someone or something else as the cause of your pain, or if you blame yourself, you will never heal. Anxiety and depression are not squashed from existence by looking outside of your mind and blame is just another form of the ego. You do want to be healed, right?

Try something that does not seem like it will work. What do you have to lose? Well, actually, you have plenty to lose - anxiety and depression. The ego inside your head that you have been relying on for the past umpteen years is not functioning properly. While it is absolutely necessary to follow your doctor's orders, take your medication, and so forth, it will be the best moment in your life when you practice no thought for two short minutes every day.

I cannot say it enough, what you are really up against - is *you and your erroneous belief system*. You and the faulty belief system are your biggest obstacles. Obviously, I do not know what your situation is, and I am not claiming any miraculous healing. The miracle is you. Maybe you went through some tougher stuff than I did. I had my fair share of hardship, but I am sure that some of you have stories that would make my story look tame.

By no means am I trying to convince you that happiness is yours for the taking regardless of what you have been through. However, the peace that passes all understanding is available to you, even during unhappy and stressful situations. There is mental freedom from anxiety and depression when we put the ego in "time out." It is the best thing I ever did. When was the last time you slept for eight hours? How about feeling peaceful again? Would you like that? When was the last day you dreaded going to sleep because your day was so flipping awesome, and you wanted it to continue? When was the last time you woke up in a state of peace?

Do not wait another minute. Start taking your life back by turning inward for the answers. The problem is the ego, not anything or anyone around you. People are forever doing things that make no sense to others but appear to make perfect sense to them. You could be doing the same. It is possible that your decision-making process is flawed. Decisions based upon flawed conditioning and paradigms will only produce a flawed outcome, thus holding you back from true peace.

Disguised in the name of safety or security, negative emotions are subconscious, invisible little decision makers that automatically determine what decision or experience is right or wrong for you. These hidden entities base their conclusions on *emotional* signals that were created in the past without first asking if you have changed your mind. Most of this irrational thinking is created as a child. You may be in a career or in a relationship that does not suit you. If you are feeling uneasiness, anxiety, or depression, it could be because your false self is processing situations based on emotions developed as a child or conditioning. This flawed thinking will keep you in a situation that does not resonate with your higher self. These hidden information processors are what is standing between you and successful relationships.

True freedom rests in alignment. Alignment is allowing the universe to work through you and trusting that it knows better about your needs, wants, desires, and how to bring them to fruition. We are smart, but not smart enough to do that. What you are actually looking for is found in alignment. The reason it is scary is because you will now be trusting in yourself through alignment. The old way was to follow directions and struggle. Alignment requires love of self-first and then the effort to act.

I have found myself in a mental place of freedom that I never knew before. I desperately want to make sure both of my children understand how to get there themselves. There is no succinct, easy way to describe it and each time I try, I use slightly different terminology. Words do not free the person from suffering. Words just point the way. It is not a "place to go" and yet that phrase may resonate with someone. Those three words might just be a catalyst for change for someone.

I am still in the process of my awakening journey. Whatever you want to call it, I think it is best to describe it now before I get to a place where I cannot explain the process because I am completely on the other side. While I am still on my personal journey, I have, however, made a complete transition to mental freedom. At any time, I am able to go to a place of complete peace. So far, none of life's challenges have been able to take away my freedom of choice. I am not, however, on autopilot. My mind sometimes wanders to the "dark side." I occasionally face a wave of anxiety. However, it is no longer debilitating, nor does it last longer than a few seconds.

Life is too short not to share this. If you are suffering from severe, chronic anxiety, like I was, there is relief. At any time, you can choose the peace that passes all understanding. It is refreshing and energizing. There is no magic pill or potion. It is a simple technique that starts with two minutes of practice.

It is a lovely position to live life from a place of completeness. With a clear direction for life, one can finally feel safe, secure, and free on every level. This is a wonderful feeling and very attainable. You got this!

EPILOGUE

I was inspired to write, *Stop Thinking* from a place of no thought that lives deep within me. I routinely followed encouragement of the divine wisdom I felt during the gaps of my habitual thinking, and the following anecdote is no exception.

Recently, in the early hours before dawn, I awoke from a deep sleep. I was compelled to leave the warmth of my bed to sit outside under the stars of the vast, Las Vegas sky. I followed my inner promptings all the while keeping the inner peace of no thought. I brought my computer with me and sat typing for hours. Pages and pages of this book flowed from me once I followed the inspiration and directions within.

I now understand that writing this book was a sort of quid pro quo. When I reflect on my life, I clearly see that this book was not written by me during the last few months. Rather, this book was written through me, and its content was being developed from my birth. It is very evident that this book has always been there, waiting to come through me, as if the life I lived needed to unfold exactly as it did for me to be at the peaceful place I am now.